143.32

CISCO CERTIFIED NETWORK

CCNA TEST YOURSELF

Personal Testing Center

CCNA TEST YOURSELF
Personal Testing Center

Syngress Media, Inc.

Osborne/McGraw-Hill
Berkeley New York St. Louis San Francisco
Auckland Bogotá Hamburg London Madrid
Mexico City Milan Montreal New Delhi Panama City
Paris São Paulo Singapore Sydney
Tokyo Toronto

Osborne/**McGraw-Hill**
2600 Tenth Street
Berkeley, California 94710
U.S.A.

For information on translations or book distributors outside the U.S.A., or to arrange bulk
purchase discounts for sales promotions, premiums, or fund-raisers, please contact
Osborne/**McGraw-Hill** at the above address.

CCNA TEST YOURSELF Personal Testing Center

1234567890 DOC DOC 90198765432109

ISBN 0-07-211950-0

Publisher
Brandon A. Nordin

**Associate Publisher and
Editor-in-Chief**
Scott Rogers

Acquisitions Editor
Gareth Hancock

Project Editor
Mark Karmendy

Editorial Assistant
Tara Davis

Copy Editor
Kathleen Faughnan

Technical Editor
Richard Hornbaker

Editorial Management
Syngress Media, Inc.

Proofreaders
Linda and Paul Medoff

Computer Designer
Jean Butterfield

Illustrators
Beth Young
Bob Hansen

Series Design
Roberta Steele

Cover Design
Regan Honda

From Global Knowledge

At Global Knowledge we strive to support the multiplicity of learning styles required by our students to achieve success as technical professionals. In this testing product, it is our intention to offer the reader a valuable tool for successful completion of the CCNA Certification Exam.

As the world's largest IT training company, Global Knowledge is uniquely positioned to offer these books. The expertise gained each year from providing instructor-led training to hundreds of thousands of students worldwide has been captured in book form to enhance your learning experience. We hope that the quality of these books demonstrates our commitment to your lifelong learning success. Whether you choose to learn through the written word, computer-based training, Web delivery, or instructor-led training, Global Knowledge is committed to providing you the very best in each of those categories. For those of you who know Global Knowledge, or those of you who have just found us for the first time, our goal is to be your lifelong competency partner.

Thank you for the opportunity to serve you. We look forward to serving your needs again in the future.

Warmest regards,

Duncan Anderson
President and Chief Operating Officer, Global Knowledge

The Global Knowledge Advantage

Global Knowledge has a global delivery system for its products and services. The company has 28 subsidiaries, and offers its programs through a total of 60+ locations. No other vendor can provide consistent services across a geographic area this large. Global Knowledge is the largest independent information technology education provider, offering programs on a variety of platforms. This enables our multi-platform and multi-national customers to obtain all of their programs from a single vendor. The company has developed the unique CompetusTM Framework software tool and methodology which can quickly reconfigure courseware to the proficiency level of a student on an interactive basis. Combined with self-paced and on-line programs, this technology can reduce the time required for training by prescribing content in only the deficient skills areas. The company has fully automated every aspect of the education process, from registration and follow-up, to "just-in-time" production of courseware. Global Knowledge, through its Enterprise Services Consultancy, can customize programs and products to suit the needs of an individual customer.

Global Knowledge Classroom Education Programs

The backbone of our delivery options is classroom-based education. Our modern, well-equipped facilities staffed with the finest instructors offer programs in a wide variety of information technology topics, many of which lead to professional certifications.

Custom Learning Solutions

This delivery option has been created for companies and governments that value customized learning solutions. For them, our consultancy-based approach of developing targeted education solutions is most effective at helping them meet specific objectives.

Self-Paced and Multimedia Products

This delivery option offers self-paced program titles in interactive CD-ROM, videotape and audio tape programs. In addition, we offer custom development of interactive multimedia courseware to customers and partners. Call us at 1 (888) 427-4228.

Electronic Delivery of Training

Our network-based training service delivers efficient competency-based, interactive training via the World Wide Web and organizational intranets. This leading-edge delivery option provides a custom learning path and "just-in-time" training for maximum convenience to students.

ARG

American Research Group (ARG), a wholly-owned subsidiary of Global Knowledge, one of the largest worldwide training partners of Cisco Systems, offers a wide range of internetworking, LAN/WAN, Bay Networks, FORE Systems, IBM, and UNIX courses. ARG offers hands on network training in both instructor-led classes and self-paced PC-based training.

Global Knowledge Courses Available

Network Fundamentals

- Understanding Computer Networks
- Telecommunications Fundamentals I
- Telecommunications Fundamentals II
- Understanding Networking Fundamentals
- Implementing Computer Telephony Integration
- Introduction to Voice Over IP
- Introduction to Wide Area Networking
- Cabling Voice and Data Networks
- Introduction to LAN/WAN protocols
- Virtual Private Networks
- ATM Essentials

Network Security & Management

- Troubleshooting TCP/IP Networks
- Network Management
- Network Troubleshooting
- IP Address Management
- Network Security Administration
- Web Security
- Implementing UNIX Security
- Managing Cisco Network Security
- Windows NT 4.0 Security

IT Professional Skills

- Project Management for IT Professionals
- Advanced Project Management for IT Professionals
- Survival Skills for the New IT Manager
- Making IT Teams Work

LAN/WAN Internetworking

- Frame Relay Internetworking
- Implementing T1/T3 Services
- Understanding Digital Subscriber Line (xDSL)
- Internetworking with Routers and Switches
- Advanced Routing and Switching
- Multi-Layer Switching and Wire-Speed Routing
- Internetworking with TCP/IP
- ATM Internetworking
- OSPF Design and Configuration
- Border Gateway Protocol (BGP) Configuration

Authorized Vendor Training

Cisco Systems

- Introduction to Cisco Router Configuration
- Advanced Cisco Router Configuration
- Installation and Maintenance of Cisco Routers
- Cisco Internetwork Troubleshooting
- Cisco Internetwork Design
- Cisco Routers and LAN Switches
- Catalyst 5000 Series Configuration
- Cisco LAN Switch Configuration
- Managing Cisco Switched Internetworks
- Configuring, Monitoring, and Troubleshooting Dial-Up Services
- Cisco AS5200 Installation and Configuration
- Cisco Campus ATM Solutions

Bay Networks

- Bay Networks Accelerated Router Configuration
- Bay Networks Advanced IP Routing
- Bay Networks Hub Connectivity
- Bay Networks Accelar 1xxx Installation and Basic Configuration
- Bay Networks Centillion Switching

FORE Systems

- FORE ATM Enterprise Core Products
- FORE ATM Enterprise Edge Products
- FORE ATM Theory
- FORE LAN Certification

Operating Systems & Programming

Microsoft

- Introduction to Windows NT
- Microsoft Networking Essentials
- Windows NT 4.0 Workstation
- Windows NT 4.0 Server
- Advanced Windows NT 4.0 Server
- Windows NT Networking with TCP/IP
- Introduction to Microsoft Web Tools
- Windows NT Troubleshooting
- Windows Registry Configuration

UNIX

- UNIX Level I
- UNIX Level II
- Essentials of UNIX and NT Integration

Programming

- Introduction to JavaScript
- Java Programming
- PERL Programming
- Advanced PERL with CGI for the Web

Web Site Management & Development

- Building a Web Site
- Web Site Management and Performance
- Web Development Fundamentals

High Speed Networking

- Essentials of Wide Area Networking
- Integrating ISDN
- Fiber Optic Network Design
- Fiber Optic Network Installation
- Migrating to High Performance Ethernet

DIGITAL UNIX

- UNIX Utilities and Commands
- DIGITAL UNIX v4.0 System Administration
- DIGITAL UNIX v4.0 (TCP/IP) Network Management
- AdvFS, LSM, and RAID Configuration and Management
- DIGITAL UNIX TruCluster Software Configuration and Management
- UNIX Shell Programming Featuring Kornshell
- DIGITAL UNIX v4.0 Security Management
- DIGITAL UNIX v4.0 Performance Management
- DIGITAL UNIX v4.0 Intervals Overview

DIGITAL OpenVMS

- OpenVMS Skills for Users
- OpenVMS System and Network Node Management I
- OpenVMS System and Network Node Management II
- OpenVMS System and Network Node Management III
- OpenVMS System and Network Node Operations
- OpenVMS for Programmers
- OpenVMS System Troubleshooting for Systems Managers
- Configuring and Managing Complex VMScluster Systems
- Utilizing OpenVMS Features from C
- OpenVMS Performance Management
- Managing DEC TCP/IP Services for OpenVMS
- Programming in C

Hardware Courses

- AlphaServer 1000/1000A Installation, Configuration and Maintenance
- AlphaServer 2100 Server Maintenance
- AlphaServer 4100, Troubleshooting Techniques and Problem Solving

ABOUT THE CONTRIBUTORS

About Syngress Media

Syngress Media creates books and software for Information Technology professionals seeking skill enhancement and career advancement. Its products are designed to comply with vendor and industry standard course curricula, and are optimized for certification exam preparation. You can contact Syngress via the Web at http://www.syngress.com.

About the Contributors

Melissa Craft, CCNA, MCSE, and MCNE, is a consulting engineer for MicroAge, a dynamic systems integration company in Phoenix, AZ. Melissa handles internetwork systems design for complex or global network projects, concentrating on infrastructure and messaging. She has a bachelor's degree from the University of Michigan. During her career, she has obtained several certifications: CCNA, MCSE, CNE-3, CNE-4, CNE-GW, MCNE, and Citrix. Melissa Craft is a member of the IEEE, the Society of Women Engineers, and American Mensa, Ltd.

Richard D. Hornbaker, CCIE, MCSE, and MCNE, is a consultant with the Forté Consulting Group, based in Phoenix, Arizona. He specializes in large-scale routing and switching projects for Fortune 500 companies. Recent projects include a 12,000-node campus network using a combination of routing, switching, and ATM. Richard is currently designing the network for a major corporate merger. Richard has over ten years of internetworking experience and holds several certifications: CCIE, MCSE, and MCNE. His skills are diverse, ranging from operating systems and software, to telephony systems and data networks. Protocol analysis and troubleshooting are among his strong suits.

Robert Aschermann, MCP, MCT, and MCSE + Internet, who authored Chapter 3, "The Career Center," has been an IS professional for nearly ten years. During his career, he has worked in technical support, systems design, consulting, and training. Rob has been an MCSE for almost three years, and has passed fifteen Microsoft certification exams. Currently

Rob works as a recruiter, trainer and consultant for Empower Trainers & Consultants, one of Microsoft's oldest and largest Authorized Technical Education Centers (ATEC). He frequently lectures at universities and job fairs on job search issues. He holds a degree in Management Systems from the University of Missouri at Rolla, as well as an M.B.A. from Baker University.

Paul Schmidt, who provided software development, has been messing about with computers since getting his hands on an Altair in 1976. He has done time at a number of software companies including Phoenix Technologies, Microsoft, America Online, and Sybase. Paul is currently an independent consultant in Windows programming and Internet Technologies. He can be reached at prs@key-dev.com or http://www.key-dev.com.

ACKNOWLEDGMENTS

We would like to thank the following people:

- **Paul Schmidt** for his astute coding and **Donnie Maurer** for his design.

CONTENTS

The Personal Training Center is part of a suite of certification tools from Global Knowledge Certification Press. While it functions as a standalone test preparation tool, it is also indexed to the best-selling Global Knowledge Certification Press Study Guides. Each testing section has a corresponding chapter in the *Cisco Certified Network Associate Study Guide*.

This booklet's purpose is two-fold: It serves as an introduction to the *Personal Testing Center* software, and it contains advice and information that certification candidates will find helpful.

In Part I, you will find a complete guide to the CCNA exam and to the *CCNA Test Yourself Personal Testing Center*. Chapter 1 offers you information on taking and preparing for the CCNA test. Chapter 2, "The CCNA Exam Buster," tells you which of the two CCNA tests are likely to be the most difficult and identifies which portions of each test are the most challenging to prepare for. Chapter 3 is "The Career Center." It discusses the techniques for a successful job search and offers advice and hints from a recruiter's perspective.

Chapter 4 is a brief guide to the *Personal Testing Center* software and how to use it to test yourself and to study for the CCNA exam.

Finally, Chapter 5 is a short resource guide to other study aides, available from various sources.

In addition, throughout the booklet, you will find notes and hints on various subjects:

CCNA
@dvice

CCNA Advice *These are hints for effective studying and test taking, written by someone who has taken a lot of tests!*

recruiter
@dvice

Recruiter Advice *These are tips to career planning: the job search, the interview, and other techniques necessary for a successful job search.*

CCNA Online *These notes provide you with the URLs to Web sites and mailing lists where you can find constantly updated and ever-changing information on the CCNA and other Cisco certifications.*

Exam Watch *These notes call attention to information about the exam and its potential pitfalls. These helpful hints are written by CCNA certified professionals—who better than to tell you what to worry about?*

Part II of the book contains three complete chapters of Osborne's best-selling *Cisco Certified Network Associate Study Guide*. In these chapters, you will find information on the following:

- **Introduction to Networking** contains information on the Internetworking Model, the physical, data link, network, and transport layers.

- **Getting Started with Cisco IOS Software** covers user and privileged modes, router basics, and initial configuration.

- **IP Addressing** covers IP addresses, subnetting and subnet masks, complex subnetting, and configuring IP addresses with Cisco IOS.

Part I

The Personal Testing Center

I

How to Take a Cisco Certification Examination

This chapter covers the importance of your CCNA certification and prepares you for taking the actual examination. It gives you a few pointers on methods of preparing for the exam, including how to study register, what to expect, and what to do on exam day.

Catch the Wave!

Congratulations on your pursuit of Cisco certification! In this fast-paced world of networking, few certifications compare to the value of Cisco's program.

The networking industry has virtually exploded in recent years, accelerated by nonstop innovation and the Internet's popularity. Cisco has stayed at the forefront of this tidal wave, maintaining a dominant role in the industry.

Since the networking industry is highly competitive and evolving technology only increases in its complexity, the rapid growth of the networking industry has created a vacuum of qualified people. There simply aren't enough skilled networking people to meet the demand. Even the most experienced professionals must keep current with the latest technology in order to provide the skills that the industry demands. That's where Cisco certification programs can help networking professionals succeed as they pursue their careers.

Cisco started its certification program many years ago, offering only the designation of Cisco Certified Internetwork Expert, or CCIE. Through the CCIE program, Cisco provided a means to meet the growing demand for experts in the field of networking. However, the CCIE tests are brutal, with a failure rate over 80 percent. (Fewer than five percent of candidates pass on their first attempt.) As you might imagine, very few people ever attain CCIE status.

In early 1998, Cisco recognized the need for intermediate certifications, and several new programs were created. Four intermediate certifications were added: CCNA (Cisco Certified Network Associate), CCNP (Cisco Certified Network Professional), CCDA (Cisco Certified Design Associate), and CCDP (Cisco Certified Design Professional). Two specialties were also created for the CCIE program: WAN Switching and ISP Dial-up.

I would encourage you to take beta tests when they are available. Not only do the beta exams cost less than the final exams (some are even free!), you will also, if you pass the beta, receive credit for passing the exam. If you don't pass the beta, you will have seen every question in the pool of available questions and can use this information when preparing to take the exam for the second time. Remember to jot down important information immediately after the exam, if you didn't pass. You will have to do this after leaving the exam area, since materials written during the exam are retained by the testing center. This information can be helpful when you need to determine which areas of the exam were most challenging for you as you study for the subsequent test.

Why Vendor Certification?

Over the years, vendors have created their own certification programs because of industry demand. This demand arises when the marketplace needs skilled professionals and an easy way to identify them. Vendors benefit because it promotes people skilled in their product. Professionals benefit because it boosts their careers. Employers benefit because it helps them identify qualified people.

In the networking industry, technology changes too often and too quickly to rely on traditional means of certification, such as universities and trade associations. Because of the investment and effort required to keep network certification programs current, vendors are the only organizations suited to keep pace with the changes. In general, such vendor certification programs are excellent, with most of them requiring a solid foundation in the essentials, as well as their particular product line.

Corporate America has come to appreciate these vendor certification programs and the value they provide. Employers recognize that certifications, like university degrees, do not guarantee a level of knowledge, experience or performance; rather, they establish a baseline for comparison. By seeking to hire vendor-certified employees, a company can assure itself that, not only has it found a person skilled in networking, but it has also hired a person skilled in the specific products the company uses.

Technical professionals have also begun to realize the value of certification and the impact it can have on their careers. By completing a certification program, professionals gain an endorsement of their skills from a major industry source. This endorsement can boost their current position and makes finding the next job even easier. Often, a certification determines whether a first interview is even granted.

Today, a certification may place you ahead of the pack. Tomorrow, it will be a necessity to keep from being left in the dust.

CCNA advice

Signing up for an exam has become more effortless with the new Web-based test registration system. To sign up for either of the CCNA exams, access http://www.2test.com and register for the Cisco Career Certification path. You will need to get an Internet account and password, if you do not already have one for 2test.com. Just select the option for first time registration, and the Web site will walk you through that process. The registration wizard even provides maps to the testing centers, something that is not available when calling Sylvan Prometric on the telephone.

Cisco's Certification Program

As mentioned previously, Cisco now has six certifications for the Routing and Switching career track, and four certifications for the WAN Switching career track. While Cisco recommends a series of courses for each of these certifications, they are not required. Ultimately, certification is dependent upon a candidate passing a series of exams. With the right experience and study materials, each of these exams can be passed without taking the associated class. Table 1-1 shows the various Cisco certifications and tracks.

TABLE 1-1   Cisco Certifications

Track	Certification	Acronym
Routing and Switching: Network Support	Cisco Certified Network Associate	CCNA
Routing and Switching: Network Support	Cisco Certified Network Professional	CCNP

TABLE 1-1	Cisco Certifications *(continued)*

Track	Certification	Acronym
Routing and Switching: Network Support	Cisco Certified Internetwork Expert (Routing and Switching)	CCIE-R/S
Routing and Switching: Network Support	Cisco Certified Internetwork Expert (ISP Dial Technology)	CCIE-ISP Dial
Routing and Switching: Network Design	Cisco Certified Design Associate	CCDA
Routing and Switching: Network Design	Cisco Certified Design Professional	CCDP
WAN Switching: Network Support	Cisco Certified Network Associate—WAN switching	CCNA-WAN Switching
WAN Switching: Network Support	Cisco Certified Network Professional—WAN switching	CCNP-WAN Switching
WAN Switching: Network Support	Cisco Certified Internetwork Expert—WAN Switching	CCIE-WAN Switching
WAN Switching: Network Design	Cisco Certified Design Professional—WAN Switching	CCDP-WAN Switching

Figure 1-1 shows Cisco's Routing and Switching track, with both the Network Design and Network Support paths. The CCNA is the foundation of the Routing and Switching track, after which candidates can pursue either the Network Design path to CCDA and CCDP, or the Network Support path to CCNP and CCIE.

Table 1-2 shows a matrix of the exams required for each Cisco certification. Note that candidates have the choice of taking either the single Foundation R/S exam, or the set of three ACRC, CLSC, and CMTD exams—all four exams are not required.

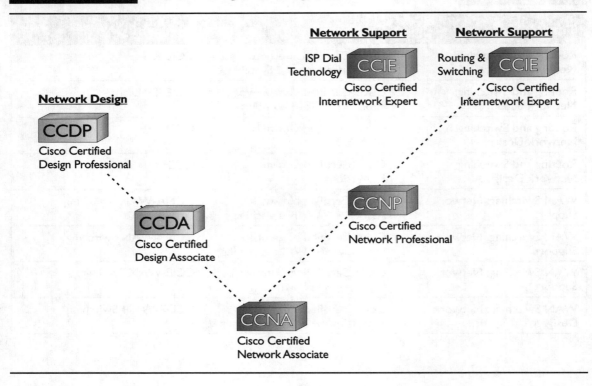

FIGURE 1-1   Cisco's Routing and Switching certification track

TABLE 1-2   Examinations Required for Cisco Certifications

Exam Name	Exam #	CCNA	CCDA	CCNP	CCDP	CCIE
CCNA 1.0	640-407	x	x	x	x	
CDS 1.0	9E0-004		x		x	
Foundation R/S	640-409			x	x	

TABLE 1-2		Examinations Required for Cisco Certifications *(continued)*				
Exam Name	**Exam #**	**CCNA**	**CCDA**	**CCNP**	**CCDP**	**CCIE**
ACRC	640-403			x	x	
CLSC	640-404			x	x	
CMTD	640-405			x	x	
CIT 3.0	640-406			x		
CIT 4.0	640-440			x		
CID	640-025				x	
CCIE R/S Qualifying						x
CCIE Lab						x

You may hear veterans refer to this CCIE R/S Qualifying Exam as the "Cisco Drake test." This is a carryover from the early days, when Sylvan Prometric's name was Drake Testing Centers, and Cisco only had the one exam.

CCNA
⊙nline

In addition to finding the technical objectives being tested for each exam, you will find more useful information on Cisco's Web site at http://www.cisco.com/warp/public/10/wwtraining/certprog.
You will find information on becoming certified, exam-specific information, sample test questions, and the latest news on Cisco certification. This is the most important site you will find on your journey to becoming Cisco certified.

CCNA advice: When I find myself stumped answering multiple-choice questions, I use my scratch paper to write down the two or three answers I consider the strongest, and then underlining the answer I feel is most likely correct. Here is an example of what my scratch paper looks like when I've gone through the test once:

21. B or <u>C</u>
33. <u>A</u> or C

This is extremely helpful when you mark the question and continue on. You can then return to the question and immediately pick up your thought process where you left off. Use this technique to avoid having to reread and rethink questions.
You will also need to use your scratch paper during complex, text-based scenario questions to create visual images to better understand the question. For example, during the CCNA exam you will need to draw multiple networks and the connections between them. By drawing the layout while you are interpreting the answer, you may find a hint that you would not have found without your own visual aid. This technique is especially helpful if you are a visual learner.

Computer-Based Testing

In a perfect world, you would be assessed for your true knowledge of a subject, not simply how you respond to a series of test questions. But life isn't perfect, and it just isn't practical to evaluate everyone's knowledge on a one-to-one basis. (Cisco actually does have a one-to-one evaluation, but it's reserved for the CCIE Laboratory exam, and the waiting list is quite long.)

For the majority of its certifications, Cisco evaluates candidates using a computer-based testing service operated by Sylvan Prometric. This service is quite popular in the industry, and it is used for a number of vendor certification programs, including Novell's CNE and Microsoft's MCSE. Thanks to Sylvan Prometric's large number of facilities, exams can be administered worldwide, generally in the same town as a prospective candidate.

For the most part, Sylvan Prometric exams work similarly from vendor to vendor. However, there is an important fact to know about Cisco's exams: they use the traditional Sylvan Prometric test format, not the newer adaptive format. This gives the candidate an advantage, since the traditional format allows answers to be reviewed and revised during the test. (The adaptive format does not.)

To discourage simple memorization, Cisco exams present a different set of questions every time the exam is administered. In the development of the exam, hundreds of questions are compiled and refined using beta testers. From this large collection, a random sampling is drawn for each test.

Each Cisco exam has a specific number of questions and test duration. Testing time is typically generous, and the time remaining is always displayed in the corner of the testing screen, along with the number of remaining questions. If time expires during an exam, the test terminates and incomplete answers are counted as incorrect.

At the end of the exam, your test is immediately graded, and the results are displayed on the screen. Scores for each subject area are also provided, but the system will not indicate which specific questions were missed. A report is automatically printed at the proctor's desk for your files. The test score is electronically transmitted back to Cisco.

In the end, this computer-based system of evaluation is reasonably fair. You might feel that one or two questions were poorly worded; this can certainly happen, but you shouldn't worry too much. Ultimately, it's all factored into the required passing score.

CCNA
advice

You will know you are coming up on a series of scenario questions because they are preceded with a blue screen, indicating that the following questions will have the same scenario, but different solutions. You must remember the scenario will be the same during the series of questions, which means you do not have to spend time reading the scenario again.

CCNA Advice

I have found it extremely helpful to put a check next to each objective as I find it is satisfied by the proposed solution. If the proposed solution does not satisfy an objective, you do not need to continue with the rest of the objectives. Once you have determined which objectives are fulfilled you can count your check marks and answer the question appropriately. This is a very effective testing technique!

CCNA Advice

Many experienced test takers do not go back and change answers unless they have a good reason to do so. Only change an answer when you feel you may have misread or misinterpreted the question the first time. Nervousness may make you second-guess every answer and talk yourself out of a correct one.

Question Types

Cisco exams pose questions in a variety of formats, most of which are discussed here. As candidates progress toward the more advanced certifications, the difficulty of the exams is intensified, both through the subject matter as well as the question formats.

True/False

The classic true/false question format is not used in the Cisco exams, for the obvious reason that a simple guess has a 50 percent chance of being correct. Instead, true/false questions are posed in multiple-choice format, requiring the candidate to identify the true or false statement from a group of selections.

Multiple Choice

Multiple choice is the primary format for questions in Cisco exams. These questions may be posed in a variety of ways.

SELECT THE CORRECT ANSWER. This is the classic multiple-choice question, where the candidate selects a single answer from a list of about four choices. In addition to the question's wording, the choices are presented in a Windows "radio button" format, where only one answer can be selected at a time.

SELECT THE 3 CORRECT ANSWERS. The multiple-answer version is similar to the single-choice version, but multiple answers must be provided. This is an "all-or-nothing" format; all the correct answers must be selected or the entire question is incorrect. In this format, the question specifies exactly how many answers must be selected. Choices are presented in a check box format, allowing more than one answer to be selected. In addition, the testing software prevents too many answers from being selected.

CCNA
Online

In order to pass these challenging exams, you may want to talk with other test takers to determine what is being tested, and what to expect in terms of difficulty. The most helpful way to communicate with other CCNA hopefuls is the Cisco mailing list. With this mailing list, you will receive e-mail every day from other members discussing everything imaginable concerning Cisco networking equipment and certification. Access this address, http://www.cisco.com/warp/public/ 84/1.html to learn how to subscribe to this wealth of information.

CCNA
Online

Make it easy on yourself and find some "brain dumps." These are notes about the exam from test takers, which indicate the most difficult concepts tested, what to look out for, and sometimes even what not to bother studying. Several of these can be found at http://www.dejanews.com. Simply do a search for CCNA and browse the recent postings. Another good resource can be found at http://www.groupstudy.com.

CCNA
Advice

In addition to gathering enough reading material for the CCNA exam, we strongly recommend you spend plenty of time using the Personal Testing Center to simulate the actual testing environment. As we indicated earlier in the section on Question Types, the Cisco exam questions are not simple multiple choice. Understanding the various types of questions that you will see during the real exam is a very important feature of the Personal Testing Center.

SELECT ALL THAT APPLY.   The open-ended version is the most difficult multiple-choice format, since the candidate does not know how many answers should be selected. As with the multiple-answer version, all the correct answers must be selected to gain credit for the question. If too many answers are selected, no credit is given. This format presents choices in check box format, but the testing software does not advise the candidates whether they've selected the correct number of answers.

Freeform Response

Freeform responses are prevalent in Cisco's advanced exams, particularly where the subject focuses on router configuration and commands. In the freeform format, no choices are provided. Instead, the test prompts for user input and the candidate must type the correct answer. This format is similar to an essay question, except the response must be very specific, allowing the computer to evaluate the answer.

For example, the question

Type the command for viewing routes learned via the EIGRP protocol.

requires the answer

```
show ip route eigrp
```

For safety's sake, you should completely spell out router commands, rather than using abbreviations. In the above example, the abbreviated command SH IP ROU EI works on a real router, but might be counted wrong by the testing software. The freeform response questions are almost always commands used in the Cisco IOS.

**CCNA
ⓐdvice**

Even though the CCNA certification is not required for CCIE certification, it is recommended that the CCNA certification be completed first. The CCNA test covers a lot of the same subjects as the CCIE test and gives you some basic groundwork for getting the next level of certification.

Fill in the Blank

Fill-in-the-blank questions are less common in Cisco exams. They may be presented in multiple-choice or freeform response format.

Exhibits

Exhibits accompany many exam questions, usually showing a network diagram or a router configuration. These exhibits are displayed in a separate window, which is opened by clicking the Exhibit button at the bottom of the screen. In some cases, the testing center may provide exhibits in printed format at the start of the exam.

Scenarios

While the normal line of questioning tests a candidate's "book knowledge," scenarios add a level of complexity. Rather than just asking technical questions, they apply the candidate's knowledge to real-world situations.

Scenarios generally consist of one or two paragraphs and an exhibit that describe a company's needs or network configuration. This description is followed by a series of questions and problems that challenge the candidate's ability to address the situation. Scenario-based questions are commonly found in exams relating to network design, but they appear to some degree in each of the Cisco exams.

Exam Objectives for the CCNA

Cisco has a clear set of objectives for the CCNA exam, upon which the exam questions are based. The following list gives a good summary of the things a CCNA must know how to do:

1. Identify and describe the functions of each of the seven layers of the OSI reference model.

2. Describe connection-oriented network service and connectionless network service, and identify the key differences between them.

3. Describe data-link addresses and network addresses, and identify the key differences between them.

4. Identify at least three reasons why the industry uses a layered model.

5. Define and explain the five conversion steps of data encapsulation.

6. Define flow control and describe the three basic methods used in networking.

7. List the key internetworking functions of the OSI Network layer and how they are performed in a router.

8. Differentiate between the following WAN services: Frame Relay, ISDN/LAPD, HDLC, and PPP.

9. Recognize key Frame Relay terms and features.

10. List commands to configure Frame Relay LMIs, maps, and subinterfaces.

11. List commands to monitor Frame Relay operation in the router.

12. Identify PPP operations to encapsulate WAN data on Cisco routers.

13. State a relevant use and context for ISDN networking.

14. Identify ISDN protocols, function groups, reference points, and channels.

15. Describe Cisco's implementation of ISDN BRI.

16. Log in to a router in both user and privileged modes.

17. Use the context-sensitive help facility.

18. Use the command history and editing features.

19. Use the SHOW command to examine router elements (RAM, ROM, CDP).

20. Manage configuration files from the privileged exec mode.

21. Control router passwords, identification, and banner.

22. Identify the main Cisco IOS commands for router startup.

23. Enter an initial configuration using the setup command.

24. Copy and manipulate configuration files.

25. List the commands to load Cisco IOS software from: flash memory, a TFTP server, or ROM.

26. Prepare to back up, upgrade, and load a backup Cisco IOS software image.

27. Prepare the initial configuration of your router and enable IP.

28. Monitor Novell IPX operation on the router.

29. Describe the two parts of network addressing, then identify the parts in specific protocol address examples.

30. Create the different classes of IP addresses [and subnetting].

31. Configure IP addresses.

32. Verify IP addresses.

33. List the required IPX address and encapsulation type.

34. Enable the Novell IPX protocol and configure interfaces.

35. Identify the functions of the TCP/IP transport-layer protocols.

36. Identify the functions of the TCP/IP network-layer protocols.

37. Identify the functions performed by ICMP.

38. Configure IPX access lists and SAP filters to control basic Novell traffic.

39. Add the RIP routing protocol to your configuration.

40. Add the IGRP routing protocol to your configuration.

41. Explain the services of separate and integrated multiprotocol routing.

42. List problems that each routing type encounters when dealing with topology changes and describe techniques to reduce the number of these problems.

43. Describe the benefits of network segmentation with routers.

44. Configure standard and extended access lists to filter IP traffic.

45. Monitor and verify selected access list operations on the router.

46. Describe the advantages of LAN segmentation.

47. Describe LAN segmentation using bridges.

48. Describe LAN segmentation using routers.

49. Describe LAN segmentation using switches.

50. Name and describe two switching methods.

51. Describe full- and half-duplex Ethernet operation.

52. Describe network congestion problem in Ethernet networks.

53. Describe the benefits of network segmentation with bridges.

54. Describe the benefits of network segmentation with switches.

55. Describe the features and benefits of Fast Ethernet.

56. Describe the guidelines and distance limitations of Fast Ethernet.

57. Distinguish between cut-through and store-and-forward LAN switching.

58. Describe the operation of the Spanning Tree Protocol and its benefits.

59. Describe the benefits of virtual LANs.

60. Define and describe the function of a MAC address.

Studying Techniques

First and foremost, give yourself plenty of time to study. Networking is a complex field, and you can't expect to cram what you need to know into a single study session. It is a field best learned over time, by studying a subject and then applying your knowledge. Build yourself a study schedule and stick to it, but be reasonable about the pressure you put on yourself, especially if you're studying in addition to your regular duties at work.

CCNA Advice

One easy technique to use in studying for certification exams is the 15-minutes-per-day effort. Simply study for a minimum of 15 minutes every day. It is a small but significant commitment. If you have a day where you just can't focus, then give up at 15 minutes. If you have a day where it flows completely for you, study longer. As long as you have more of the "flow days," your chances of succeeding are extremely high.

Second, practice and experiment. In networking, you need more than knowledge; you need understanding, too. You can't just memorize facts to be effective; you need to understand why events happen, how things work, and (most importantly) how they break.

The best way to gain deep understanding is to take your book knowledge to the lab. Try it out. Make it work. Change it a little. Break it. Fix it.

Snoop around "under the hood." If you have access to a network analyzer, like Network Associate's Sniffer, put it to use. You can gain amazing insight to the inner workings of a network by watching devices communicate with each other.

Unless you have a very understanding boss, don't experiment with router commands on a production router. A seemingly innocuous command can have a nasty side effect. If you don't have a lab, your local Cisco office or Cisco users group may be able to help. Many training centers also allow students access to their lab equipment during off-hours.

Another excellent way to study is through case studies. Case studies are articles or interactive discussions that offer real-world examples of how technology is applied to meet a need. These examples can serve to cement your understanding of a technique or technology by seeing it put to use. Interactive discussions offer added value because you can also pose questions of your own. User groups are an excellent source of examples, since the purpose of these groups is to share information and learn from each other's experiences.

Also not to be missed is the Cisco Networkers conference. Although renowned for its wild party and crazy antics, this conference offers a wealth of information. Held every year in cities around the world, it includes three days of technical seminars and presentations on a variety of subjects. As you might imagine, it's very popular. You have to register early to get the classes you want.

Then, of course, there is the Cisco Web site. This little gem is loaded with collections of technical documents and white papers. As you progress to more advanced subjects, you will find great value in the large number of examples and reference materials available. But be warned: You need to do a lot of digging to find the really good stuff. Often, your only option is to browse every document returned by the search engine to find exactly the one you need. This effort pays off. Most CCIEs I know have compiled six to ten binders of reference material from Cisco's site alone.

Scheduling Your Exam

The Cisco exams are scheduled by calling Sylvan Prometric directly at (800) 204-3926. For locations outside the United States, your local number can be found on Sylvan's Web site at **http://www.prometric.com**. Sylvan representatives can schedule your exam, but they don't have information about the certification programs. Questions about certifications should be directed to Cisco's training department.

The aforementioned Sylvan telephone number is specific to Cisco exams, and it goes directly to the Cisco representatives inside Sylvan. These representatives are familiar enough with the exams to find them by name, but it's best if you have the specific exam number handy when you call. After all, you wouldn't want to be scheduled and charged for the wrong exam (for example, the instructor's version, which is significantly harder).

Exams can be scheduled up to a year in advance, although it's really not necessary. Generally, scheduling a week or two ahead is sufficient to reserve the day and time you prefer. When scheduling, operators will search for testing centers in your area. For convenience, they can also tell which testing centers you've used before.

Sylvan accepts a variety of payment methods, with credit cards being the most convenient. When paying by credit card, you can even take tests the same day you call—provided, of course, that the testing center has room. (Quick scheduling can be handy, especially if you want to retake an exam immediately.) Sylvan will mail you a receipt and confirmation of your testing date, although this generally arrives after the test has been taken. If you need to cancel or reschedule an exam, remember to call at least one day before your exam, or you'll lose your test fee.

When registering for the exam, you will be asked for your ID number. This number is used to track your exam results back to Cisco. It's important that you use the same ID number each time you register, so that Cisco can follow your progress. Address information provided when you first register is also used by Cisco to ship certificates and other related material. In the USA, your Social Security Number is commonly used as your ID number. However, Sylvan can assign you a unique ID number if you prefer not to use your Social Security Number.

Table 1-3 shows the available Cisco exams and the number of questions and duration of each. This information is subject to change as Cisco revises the exams, so it's a good idea to verify the details when registering for an exam.

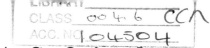
TABLE 1-3   Cisco Exam Lengths, Question Counts, and Fees

Exam Title	Exam Number	Number of Questions	Duration (minutes)	Exam Fee ($US)
Cisco Design Specialist (CDS)	9E0-004	80	180	$100
Cisco Internetwork Design (CID)	640-025	100	120	$100
Advanced Cisco Router Configuration (ACRC)	640-403	72	90	$100
Cisco LAN Switch Configuration (CLSC)	640-404	70	60	$100
Configuring, Monitoring, and Troubleshooting Dialup Services (CMTD)	640-405	64	90	$100
Cisco Internetwork Troubleshooting (CIT)*	640-406	77	105	$100
Cisco Certified Network Associate (CCNA)	640-407	70	90	$100
Foundation Routing & Switching	640-409	132	165	$100
CCIE Routing & Switching Qualification	350-001	100	120	$200
CCIE Certification Laboratory	N/A	N/A	2 days	$1000

*As of this writing, Cisco is still offering the CIT, exam 640-406, which has 69 questions and runs 60 minutes. The exam will likely retire once the new exam is established.

In addition to the regular Sylvan Prometric testing sites, Cisco also offers facilities for taking exams free of charge at each Networkers conference in the USA. As you might imagine, this option is quite popular, so reserve your exam time as soon as you arrive at the conference.

Arriving at the Exam

As with any test, you'll be tempted to cram the night before. Resist that temptation. You should know the material by this point, and if you're too groggy in the morning, you won't remember what you studied anyway. Instead, get a good night's sleep.

Arrive early for your exam; it gives you time to relax and review key facts. Take the opportunity to review your notes. If you get burned out on studying, you can usually start your exam a few minutes early. On the other hand, I don't recommend arriving late. Your test could be cancelled, or you may not be left with enough time to complete the exam.

When you arrive at the testing center, you'll need to sign in with the exam administrator. In order to sign in, you need to provide two forms of identification. Acceptable forms include government-issued IDs (for example, passport or driver's license), credit cards, and company ID badge. One form of ID must include a photograph.

Aside from a brain full of facts, you don't need to bring anything else to the exam. In fact, your brain is about all you're allowed to take into the exam. All the tests are "closed book," meaning you don't get to bring any reference materials with you. Also, you're not allowed to take any notes out of the exam room. The test administrator will provide you with paper and a pencil. Some testing centers may provide a small marker board instead.

Calculators are not allowed, so be prepared to do any necessary math (such as hex-binary-decimal conversions or subnet masks) in your head or on paper. Additional paper is available if you need it.

Leave your pager and telephone in the car, or turn them off. They only add stress to the situation, since they are not allowed in the exam room, and can sometimes still be heard if they ring outside of the room. Purses, books, and other materials must be left with the administrator before entering the exam. While in the exam room, it's important that you don't disturb other candidates; talking is not allowed during the exam.

Once in the testing room, the exam administrator logs onto your exam, and you have to verify that your ID number and the exam number are correct. If this is the first time you've taken a Cisco test, you can select a brief tutorial for the exam software. Before the test begins, you will be provided with facts about the exam, including the duration, the number of questions, and the score required for passing. Then the clock starts ticking and the fun begins.

The testing software is Windows-based, but you won't have access to the main desktop or any of the accessories. The exam is presented in full screen, with a single question per screen. Navigation buttons allow you to move forward and backward between questions. In the upper-right corner of the screen, counters show the number of questions and time remaining. Most importantly, there is a "Mark" check box in the upper-left corner of the screen—this will prove to be a critical tool in your testing technique.

Test-Taking Techniques

One of the most frequent excuses I hear for failing a Cisco exam is "poor time management." Without a plan of attack, candidates are overwhelmed by the exam or become sidetracked and run out of time. For the most part, if you are comfortable with the material, the allotted time is more than enough to complete the exam. The trick is to keep the time from slipping away during any one particular problem.

The obvious goal of an exam is to answer the questions effectively, although other aspects of the exam can distract from this goal. After taking a fair number of computer-based exams, I've naturally developed a technique for tackling the problem, which I share with you here. Of course, you still need to learn the material. These steps just help you take the exam more efficiently.

Size Up the Challenge

First, take a quick pass through all the questions in the exam. "Cherry-pick" the easy questions, answering them on the spot. Briefly read each question, noticing the type of question and the subject. As a guideline, try to spend less than 25 percent of your testing time in this pass.

This step lets you assess the scope and complexity of the exam, and it helps you determine how to pace your time. It also gives you an idea of where to find potential answers to some of the questions. Often, the answer to one question is shown in the exhibit of another. Sometimes the wording of one question might lend clues or jog your thoughts for another question.

Imagine that the following questions are posed in this order:

Question 1: Review the router configurations and network diagram in exhibit XYZ (not shown here). Which devices should be able to ping each other?

Question 2: If RIP routing were added to exhibit XYZ, which devices would be able to ping each other?

The first question seems straightforward. Exhibit XYZ probably includes a diagram and a couple of router configurations. Everything looks normal, so you decide that all devices can ping each other.

Now, consider the hint left by the Question 2. When you answered Question 1, did you notice that the configurations were missing the routing protocol? Oops! Being alert to such clues can help you catch your own mistakes.

If you're not entirely confident with your answer to a question, answer it anyway, but check the Mark box to flag it for later review. In the event that you run out of time, at least you've provided a "first guess" answer, rather than leaving it blank.

Take on the Scenario Questions

Second, go back through the entire test, using the insight you gained from the first go-through. For example, if the entire test looks difficult, you'll know better than to spend more than a minute or so on each question. Break down the pacing into small milestones; for example, "I need to answer 10 questions every 15 minutes."

At this stage, it's probably a good idea to skip past the time-consuming questions, marking them for the next pass. Try to finish this phase before you're 50–60 percent through the testing time.

By now, you probably have a good idea where the scenario questions are found. A single scenario tends to have several questions associated with it, but they aren't necessarily grouped together in the exam. Rather than rereading the scenario every time you encounter a related question, save some time and answer the questions as a group.

Tackle the Complex Problems

Third, go back through all the questions you marked for review, using the Review Marked button in the question review screen. This step includes taking a second look at all the questions you were unsure of in previous passes, as well as tackling the time-consuming ones you deferred until now. Chisel away at this group of questions until you've answered them all.

If you're more comfortable with a previously marked question, unmark it now. Otherwise, leave it marked. Work your way through the time-consuming questions now, especially those requiring manual calculations. Unmark them when you're satisfied with the answer.

By the end of this step, you've answered every question in the test, despite having reservations about some of your answers. If you run out of time in the next step, at least you won't lose points for lack of an answer. You're in great shape if you still have 10–20 percent of your time remaining.

Review Your Answers

Now you're cruising! You've answered all the questions, and you're ready to do a quality check. Take yet another pass (yes, one more) through the entire test, briefly rereading each question and your answer. Be cautious about revising answers at this point unless you're sure a change is warranted. If there's a doubt about changing the answer, I always trust my first instinct and leave the original answer intact.

Rarely are "trick" questions asked, so don't read too much into the questions. Again, if the wording of the question confuses you, leave the answer intact. Your first impression was probably right.

Be alert for last-minute clues. You're pretty familiar with nearly every question at this point, and you may find a few clues that you missed before.

The Grand Finale

When you're confident with all your answers, finish the exam by submitting it for grading. After what will seem like the longest ten seconds of your life, the testing software will respond with your score. This is usually displayed as a bar graph, showing the minimum passing score, your score, and a PASS/FAIL indicator.

If you're curious, you can review the statistics of your score at this time. Answers to specific questions are not presented; rather, questions are lumped into categories, and results are tallied for each category. This detail is also printed on a report that has been automatically printed at the exam administrator's desk.

As you leave the exam, you'll need to leave your scratch paper behind or return it to the administrator. (Some testing centers track the number of sheets you've been given, so be sure to return them all.) In exchange, you'll receive a copy of the test report.

This report will be embossed with the testing center's seal, and you should keep it in a safe place. Normally, the results are automatically transmitted to Cisco, but occasionally you might need the paper report to prove that you passed the exam. Your personnel file is probably a good place to keep this report; the file tends to follow you everywhere, and it doesn't hurt to have favorable exam results turn up during a performance review.

Retesting

If you don't pass the exam, don't be discouraged—networking is complex stuff. Try to have a good attitude about the experience, and get ready to try again. Consider yourself a little more educated. You know the format of the test a little better, and the report shows which areas you need to strengthen.

If you bounce back quickly, you'll probably remember several of the questions you might have missed. This will help you focus your study efforts in the right area. Serious go-getters will reschedule the exam for a couple days after the previous attempt, while the study material is still fresh in their mind.

Ultimately, remember that a Cisco certification is valuable because it's hard to get. After all, if anyone could get one, what value would it have? In the end, it takes a good attitude and a lot of studying, but you can do it!

2

The CCNA
Exam Buster

I n this section we will be discussing the most difficult exams offered by Cisco, and also the easiest. These conclusions are based on numerous posts from CCNAs and my own test-taking experience. Bear in mind that every Cisco exam is challenging, and any exam can cause you difficulty if you are not prepared. We will also present the recommended order for taking tests on your path to becoming a CCNA, or beyond. This recommended test-taking order represents a summation of what many CCNAs believe to be a smooth transition from one exam to another, with overlapping study material as much as possible, which means less studying for you. Keep in mind that this recommended order of study is by no means a strict guideline.

The Hardest Exam?

Only one exam is required to become a CCNA. Either the CCNA 1.0 test 640-407 or the CCNA WAN Switching test 640-410 can lead to certification. Although the hardest exam is a matter of opinion, several CCNAs have noted that the WAN Switching exam 640-410 is one of the most difficult exams they have ever taken. Since this exam is a required exam in the CCNA WAN Switching track, it is unavoidable to those who pursue that track.

The Easiest Exam?

The easiest exam is also a matter of opinion. The only remaining test to be considered the "easiest" is the CCNA 1.0 exam 640-407. Of all the tests required for further certification as a CCNP or CCDP, the CCNA 1.0 test would probably still qualify as the easiest of the total set of required exams.

CCNA 1.0

As indicated earlier, the CCNA 1.0 exam (exam 70-058) is recommended as the exam on your way to becoming a CCNA, and as the first exam on the path to CCDP or CCNP. This test is surprisingly difficult due to the complexity of the scenario questions. If this is your first Cisco exam, you may be caught off guard by the types of questions you will see. However, with time spent using the *Personal Testing Center*, you will have the opportunity to encounter scenario questions that are very indicative of what you will see on the real Cisco exam.

Although some candidates have passed the exam with only Cisco training study materials, I would not recommend use of *just* these study materials. The CCNA 1.0 exam will require quite a bit of hands-on experience, especially in the areas of installing and configuring routers and switches. It is recommended that you supplement the Cisco training materials with another book (at least) and some lab time that will give you more chances to practice and review the material, and ultimately, give you more confidence.

Toughest Topics on the Exam

The most challenging aspect of the CCNA exam for those of you who are new to networking will be the large volume of material that needs to be memorized. The following items need to be committed to memory, as they will constitute a large portion of the exam:

- Seven layers of the OSI reference model
- WAN Protocols
- Cisco Internetwork Operating System
- Network Protocols (LAN)
- Routing on "Simple" networks
- LAN Switching and segmentation

Cisco hardware is used in many Internet-attached internetworks. In fact, Cisco is well known for its use on the Internet. As a result, much of the Cisco Internetwork Operating System assumes the usage of IP (Internet Protocol). Routing subjects on the CCNA exam will require a detailed knowledge of IP addressing, subnetting, and access-lists.

exam
Watch

You should know each layer of the OSI model and the purpose for each layer. The well-known memory mnemonic, All People Seem To Need Data Processing, will be very helpful when remembering each layer of the OSI model from top to bottom: application, presentation, session, transport, network, data link, and physical.

You will also be expected to know the characteristics of each protocol layer, the various networking protocols, and when to use each in a given situation.

Memorizing the characteristics of each type of network cable and network topology may be the most challenging aspect of the exam. Many test takers quickly jot everything they can remember about cable lengths and maximum nodes per segment before the test to use for reference later in the exam. You are expected to know which network topology to use in a given situation, and most of these questions usually involve a complex scenario.

The characteristics of the various networking hardware devices must be thoroughly memorized, but questions on this topic are quite straightforward and do not involve complex scenarios. Know when to use a specific device in a given situation and the layer of the OSI model in which the device resides.

If you don't have experience with Cisco routers or switches, the exam will present quite a bit of difficulty. As a candidate for CCNA certification, you are required to know the Cisco IOS—Internetwork Operating System—that runs on all Cisco hardware. The best way to learn these commands is to use them on the hardware itself.

Table 2-1 outlines what should be your study objectives for the CCNA 1.0 exam, according to Cisco.

TABLE 2-1	CCNA Test Objectives
OSI reference model	Identify and describe the functions of each of the seven layers of the OSI reference model. Describe connection-oriented network service and connectionless network service, and identify the key differences between them. Describe data link addresses and network addresses, and identify the key differences between them. Identify at least three reasons why the industry uses a layered model. Define and explain the five conversion steps of data encapsulation. Define flow control and describe the three basic methods used in networking. List the key internetworking functions of the OSI network layer and how they are performed in a router.

TABLE 2-1	CCNA Test Objectives *(continued)*
WAN protocols	Differentiate between the following WAN services: ● Frame Relay ● ISDN ● LAPD ● HDLC ● PPP Recognize key Frame Relay terms and features: ● PVC ● SVC ● DLCI List commands to configure Frame Relay LMIs, maps, and subinterfaces. List commands to monitor Frame Relay operation in the router. Identify PPP operations to encapsulate WAN data on Cisco routers. State a relevant use and context for ISDN networking. Identify ISDN protocols, function groups, reference points, and channels. Describe Cisco's implementation of ISDN BRI.
IOS	Log in to a router in both user and privileged exec modes. Use the context-sensitive help facility. Use the command history and editing features. Examine router elements (RAM, ROM, CDP, show). Manage configuration files from the privileged exec mode. Control router passwords, identification, and banner. Identify the main Cisco IOS commands for router startup. Enter an initial configuration using the setup command. Copy and manipulate configuration files. List the commands to load Cisco IOS software from flash memory, a TFTP server, or ROM. Prepare to back up, upgrade, and load a backup Cisco IOS software image. Prepare the initial configuration of your router and enable IP.
Network protocols	Monitor Novell IPX operation on the router. Describe the two parts of network addressing; then identify the parts in specific protocol address examples. Create the different classes of IP addresses (and subnetting). Configure IP addresses. Verify IP addresses. List the required IPX address and encapsulation type. Enable the Novell IPX protocol and configure interfaces. Identify the functions of the TCP/IP transport-layer protocols. Identify the functions of the TCP/IP network-layer protocols. Identify the functions performed by ICMP. Configure IPX access lists and SAP filters to control basic Novell traffic.
Routing	Add the RIP routing protocol to your configuration. Add the IGRP routing protocol to your configuration. Explain the services of separate and integrated multiprotocol routing. List problems that each routing type encounters when dealing with topology changes and describe techniques to reduce the number of these problems. Describe the benefits of network segmentation with routers.

TABLE 2-1	CCNA Test Objectives (continued)
Network security	Configure standard and extended access lists to filter IP traffic. Monitor and verify selected access list operations on the router.
LAN switching	Describe the advantages of LAN segmentation. Describe LAN segmentation using bridges. Describe LAN segmentation using routers. Describe LAN segmentation using switches. Name and describe two switching methods. Describe full- and half-duplex Ethernet operation. Describe network congestion problem in Ethernet networks. Describe the benefits of network segmentation with bridges. Describe the benefits of network segmentation with switches. Describe the features and benefits of Fast Ethernet. Describe the guidelines and distance limitations of Fast Ethernet. Distinguish between cut-through and store-and-forward LAN switching. Describe the operation of the Spanning Tree Protocol and its benefits. Describe the benefits of virtual LANs. Define and describe the function of a MAC address.

The CCNA certification is new, compared to the established CCIE certification. Cisco created the CCNA certification to provide a first step toward further Cisco certifications, including the CCIE. As a result, much of the data available for the CCIE certification is applicable to CCNA. The best place to find this information is at http://www.groupstudy.com.

When asking CCNA testers what they would suggest you study for the exam, the most common reply is access lists. The access list functionality in a Cisco router is used to filter traffic. There are access lists for different protocols, such as IPX and TCP/IP. Each has a slightly different IOS configuration command and numbered range. This can be difficult enough for the test as it is, but it gets worse. For example, the most tricky thing about an access list is the implied "Deny Any" command. The implied "Deny Any" command will filter out all traffic that is not explicitly permitted in the access list. This means that an access list that has a single Permit statement would then deny all other traffic—even though it did not include a single Deny statement! So, know your access lists before taking that exam.

The second most difficult exam topic reported by testers is the IP addressing. It is not always tested on its own but must be known to answer questions about IOS commands to assign an address to a router interface, or otherwise configure a router. Other questions assume that you will know IP classes, the way to subnet, and allowed addresses for that subnet in order to answer a question on a network design configuration.

CCNA-WAN Switching

The CCNA-WAN Switching test starts you out on the WAN Switching career certification track. The WAN Switching certification ensures that you have the skills required to configure, operate, troubleshoot, and manage WAN switched networks. The entire track will cover

- Knowledge of WAN protocols such as Frame Relay and ATM
- Media and telephony transmission techniques, including error detection and multiplexing such as Time Division Multiplexing (TDM)
- Knowledge of Cisco-specific technologies, including WAN switch platforms, applications, architectures, and interfaces
- Knowledge of service provider technology, including packet encapsulation and network-to-network interconnections

If you have decided to take the alternate track of WAN Switching, then you will be studying for exam 640-410: CCNA-WAN Switching. It is unlikely that anyone will be taking both the CCNA 1.0 and the CCNA-WAN Switching exams. If you do, however, you will not have to study as much as you did for the CCNA exam because most of the concepts presented in the CCNA exam also apply to the WAN Switching exam.

Toughest Topics on the Exam

Many CCNAs remember the WAN Switching exam as being heavily geared toward connectivity configuration issues on a Cisco router. Table 2-2 outlines what should be your study objectives for the WAN Switching exam.

TABLE 2-2	WAN Switching Test Objectives
OSI reference model	Identify and describe the functions of each of the seven layers of the OSI reference model. Describe connection-oriented network service and connectionless network service, and identify the key differences between them. List the key internetworking functions of the OSI network layer and how they are performed in a router.
Install devices	Install IGX, BPX, and Axis devices. Perform setup configuration. Troubleshoot installation problems. Inventory installed cards and power supplies. Log in to the system, and identify software revision, card types, revisions, and status. Monitor environmental characteristics, and use online help.
Upgrade and configure devices	Replace defective devices. Perform upgrades to firmware and software for StrataCom, IGX, BPX, and AXIS switches. Configure the node name, system date and time, and local time zone. Display and modify control/auxiliary port configuration. Identify the IP addresses of the node.
Design WAN systems and use Strata software	Identify Cisco WAN systems and their key functions. Identify devices on a network drawing. Describe the functions of StrataView Plus and StrataView Lite network management software. List installation tool requirements. Perform a formal site survey. Unpack and inspect Cisco WAN devices. Identify equipment mounting options. Install StrataView Lite onto your laptop computer. Identify devices and connection options in network configuration drawings. Connect StrataCom WAN devices into a functioning wide-area network. Locate software and firmware files for upgrades. Upgrade the software in IGX and BPX nodes. Upgrade the firmware in IGX, BPX, and AXIS nodes. Describe how an active processor updates a standby processor. Describe what to do when the active processor fails. Upgrade an IPX node from PCC modules to NPC modules. Diagnose and repair hardware failures in the IGX, BPX, and AXIS systems. Diagnose alarm conditions in the IGX, BPX, and AXIS systems.
IGX	Identify features and functions of the IGX cards. Describe the steps to install an IGX switch in a rack. Describe how each component is installed in the IGX 8 switch. Identify features and functions of the IGX cards. Install an IGX switch in a rack. Install each component in an IGX switch.
BPX and AXIS	Identify features and functions of the BPX cards. Install a BPX chassis in a rack. Install each component in a BPX switch. Identify features and functions of the AXIS cards. Install an AXIS chassis in a rack. Install each component in an AXIS shelf. Identify normal and abnormal boosting sequences. Configure an AXIS shelf.

3

The Career Center

Y ou might be tempted to think that your work is finished once you have achieved your CCNA certification. Nothing could be further from the truth. Now that you have the certification, you need a job that is going to provide opportunities to use your certification. You might also look for a job that will allow you to obtain additional certifications. Finding that job can be difficult if you don't know where to look or what to look for.

The "Help Wanteds": Planning Your Attack

Looking at the title of this section, you might think you were going to war. Well, it's not quite as bad as that; but a job-hunting campaign, like a military campaign, should have a strategy. Many people start with the attitude that if you have no idea what you're looking for, then you won't be disappointed with what you find. There's probably some truth in that, but I would add that you probably won't find the job that's right for you, either.

I also like to use the analogy of courtship when explaining the importance of having a strategy for your search. If you've never stopped to think about your perfect mate, then chances are you don't really know what you're looking for. If you go ahead and get married anyway, you could find yourself in a marriage that is going to lead to a messy divorce or many years of unhappiness.

Getting fired or quitting a job isn't as bad as getting a divorce, but it's not much fun. In my career I've had good and bad jobs, jobs that have gone from good to bad, and jobs that have gone from bad to good. I've been hired, fired, and I've "moved on to other opportunities" (I quit). All of these changes required decisions from me, and a lot of thought had to go into those decisions.

In the next few pages, I'm going to try to help you develop a job search strategy.

(✋)
**recruiter
ⓐdvice**

Before talking to a headhunter or recruiter, put together an information packet that includes a resume, a cover letter, a skills list, a project list, and maybe even references. The more information you provide, the easier it will be for a headhunter or recruiter to place you.

The Job Search

We begin with the job search. Time seems to be the biggest factor for most folks when it comes to looking for a new job. How long is this going to take? That's a tough question. The answer depends on the market, the type of job you are looking for, and your personal situation.

The ideal situation to be in when searching for a new job is to have a job you already like. That might not make sense at first, but think about it for a minute. If you don't feel like you have to leave your current job, you aren't going to feel as much pressure to take a less than optimal new job. You will spend more time learning about new opportunities and educating yourself about what you're getting into.

With more time, you may broaden your search and consider areas or industries that you might not have considered under a time crunch. You'll feel better about holding out for a higher salary or a better signing bonus. Most importantly, you will not be rushed into a decision that is going to shape the rest of your life. You will have time to decide what you want, and then to develop a strategy for how you are going to get it.

Incidentally, recruiters love to find people who are under the gun, because recruiters know that they can get these people on board faster and at a lower cost. However, a manager will recognize that this type of person may not be around for long, because the person may be getting into a job he isn't suited for. Remember that recruiters make recommendations, but it's managers who make decisions.

If you happen to find yourself "between jobs" at the moment, don't sweat it. If you are certified, or are getting certified, the jobs are out there. Just relax and take some time to focus on your strategy. Then implement that strategy.

If you aren't currently in a job, you may actually have an advantage over someone who does have a job. You have an abundance of one of the world's most limited resources: spare time!

(🖐)
recruiter
ⓐdvice

Develop a strategy for landing your ideal job. That strategy should include defining what your ideal job is, who you need to meet to get an interview, and what you need to do to prepare for the interview.

Networking 101

You have heard someone say, "It's not what you know, but whom you know." There is some truth in that. Networking has two big benefits for you if it's done right. The first benefit is contacts. The second benefit is association.

The contacts benefit is fairly straightforward, so we'll talk about that one in a second. Let's talk about associations first, since that's the one that might not be so obvious. One very common method of networking is to join professional groups like software user groups. Even if you don't attend the meetings, you can tell people that you're a card-carrying member of the XYZ group.

If the XYZ group has a reputation for being a very technical and prestigious group, chances are your value just went up in the mind of the recruiter. By the way, you are also demonstrating the capacity to be social. Most recruiters aren't interested in even the most technically proficient people, if they can't relate to other people.

Let's say, for a moment, that you did join a users group or any type of social organization, and you actually attended the meetings. Whom might you meet there? Well, you might meet me or one of my fellow recruiters. That could prove helpful.

You might also meet MIS directors, project managers, senior technical leads, or entrepreneurs. All of these people are always on the lookout for talent—it's ingrained in them. Every time they meet someone new, the question they ask themselves is, "Could I use this person?"

If you can prompt someone to ask that question about you, and answer "yes," then you have probably just found yourself a job. At a minimum, you have gained recognition from an influential person inside the organization. That puts you about a light-year ahead of your competitors who are answering ads from the Sunday paper.

(✋)
**recruiter
@dvice**

Make yourself a list of questions before going into an interview. You don't even have to memorize them. Take notes, and press for information if you aren't satisfied with the answers. Remember that you are interviewing the company just as much as they are interviewing you.

Using Placement Services

I have mixed feelings about placement services. I think placement services are excellent vehicles for finding entry-level positions. If you have just finished your CCNA, then a placement service might be a good choice for you.

However, if you've had your CCNA for a while, or if you already have a lot of industry experience, then be careful of placement services. Most services make their money by doing a volume business. You register with the service, and the service attempts to place you in the first job request they receive for which you are qualified.

Placement services rarely take the time to investigate the jobs into which they are placing people. Many times the placement services get their lists of job positions right out of a newspaper. Many of the opportunities that you will find through placement services are temporary staffing positions.

(✋)
recruiter
@dvice

You may be interviewed by a variety of people. Some will be technical and some will be more business oriented. Match technical questions to technical people, and business questions to business people. If you can appeal to both of these groups, you have a good chance of getting a job.

This might be just what you need to build a resume. However, for an experienced individual looking for a full-time position as a senior technical lead, listing a number of temporary staffing positions on your resume may do you more harm than good.

If you choose to use a placement service, consider using one of the nationwide services like Kelly Technical Services or AeroTek. I have been impressed in the past with the speed at which these services have filled positions and with the quality of applicants that these services attract. Also, if you are willing to travel, the nationwide services may be able to find you a specific type of job.

To sum it up, my advice on placement services is not to discount them. Just make sure that the type of job you are looking for is the type of job that the service fills on a regular basis.

(✋)
**recruiter
@dvice**

To help you define what your ideal job is, ask your peers about various jobs they have had. Ask a headhunter or recruiter what kinds of jobs are available and what kinds of people get those jobs. Career counselors can also help. When searching for a job, try to expand your search to include other areas of the country or other industries. Often, companies in other industries will pay well for a set of skills that is not usually found in that industry.

Going Online

By now, I hope I don't need to tell you that you can find a wealth of information on the Internet. This includes company marketing information, securities exchange information, and recruiting information. Almost all of the Fortune 500 companies, and many of the smaller ones, provide a way to submit resumes, either through an e-mail address or through a Web form.

If you submit your resume through e-mail, be sure that you clearly indicate what file format it's in. Pick something common like RTF format or Microsoft Word 6.0/95 format. When you submit your resume via e-mail, you can be reasonably sure that someone is going to print it out and read it.

Here's a situation in which you need to plan for the least common denominator. All your high-resolution color graphics, watermarks, and textures may look great at home; but, when printed on the high-volume laser printer at the recruiter's office, they become distracting. Guess what happens to resumes that are distracting and hard to read. That's right—straight into the trash. I've thrown away dozens of resumes because they were just too much work to read.

When submitting your resume via an online form, you need a slightly different strategy. Think keywords. There's a good chance that all of that information you are entering is being stored in a database. At some point, someone is going to run a query against that database that goes something like this, "Show me all of the CCNAs with at least THREE YEARS' WORK EXPERIENCE."

You've got to get as many keywords as you can into the information you are entering in the database. That way, your name will come up more often. As you can imagine, trying to maximize keywords can lead to some pretty hilarious text, but it works. It also demonstrates that you understand how computer systems work. That isn't lost on recruiters.

If you happen to be just what a company is looking for, then submitting your resume online might be a good idea. However, it's been my experience that submitting a resume online isn't much better than mailing in a resume to the attention of the personnel director.

I'm not fond of this method, because it lacks a certain personal touch. Also, you really have no idea who is receiving your resume. It might be someone in the personnel department at a company, or it might be someone at a placement office that has the contract for the company you are interested in.

recruiter ⓐdvice

Never pass up an opportunity to meet someone in the industry. Network as much as possible. Attend professional conferences and user group meetings. Always have a few business cards on hand, and be prepared for an informal, on-the-spot interview.

Whenever I submit my resume, I always identify the job I'm looking for, then I find out who is responsible for filling that position. This often requires a little inside knowledge. Try to find someone in the organization who will give you an exact job title and the name of a manager responsible for filling that position.

An excellent source for this type of information is ex-employees. Most will be more than happy to give you the inside scoop. They will probably also be willing to tell you what to look out for. Finding an ex-employee and taking him or her out to lunch may be one of the best investments you ever make.

After a personal contact, such as a phone call or a lunch appointment, I then submit my resume to that person. That person then becomes my sponsor. He or she passes my resume on to whoever needs to see it, hopefully with some positive remarks. That is a level of personal contact that just can't be achieved through an online submittal process.

recruiter ⓐdvice

If you are looking for an entry-level job, or if you have just recently completed your certification and need to build some practical skills, think about using a placement service. Often a placement service can find an entry-level position that will work for you in just a few days.

recruiter @dvice

Never pay someone to find you a job. Professionals in this industry are paid a commission by the company. Ask your headhunter how he or she collects a fee. It's in your best interest if the headhunter is being paid a finder's fee that is a percentage of your new salary.

One other place to start online is by posting your resume in a resume database. These databases will let anyone looking for almost any type of job (although some resume databases are industry-specific) post a resume for free. The online databases have a bonus! They usually have a matching database of available jobs that you can browse through. These jobs are listed from all over the world; so, if you are looking for a job in another city, state, province, or country, you may find it here.

These Web sites typically make their money from advertisers and/or from charging fees to recruiting companies to browse the database. Because some of the Web sites charge fees, and because some people prefer one Web site over another, it is best to post your resume on several.

Before you start posting your resume, you will first need to save it in ASCII format. Most Web databases will only store a simple ASCII text file. These sites will use a search engine using Web technology to browse for the keywords in the resume. Other Web sites will ask you to complete a resume online using their form. They will have a more sophisticated indexing of your resume for better search results. If you have already created a resume in ASCII text, it is a simple task of copy and paste from the text file to the Web form.

The only other prerequisite to posting a resume online is that you *must* have an e-mail address. Nearly every site will require an e-mail address to register you as a user who can post a resume and will use it to e-mail you your password. Some sites use the e-mail address to notify you of the impending purging of your resume from the online database.

The following are some of the top sites on which to post a resume:

- The Monster Board: http://www.monster.com
- CareerMosaic: http://www.careermosaic.com
- The Online Career Center: http://www.occ.com

Getting the Advice of Peers

Once you have identified a company that you want to work for, you need to get the lay of the land. You need to gather intelligence. Try to make some contacts within the company, and try to meet some people who have interviewed with the company before. This is usually easier said than done, but you can get some really valuable information.

Ask around. You might just get lucky and find someone who has successfully, or unsuccessfully, done what you are trying to do. Try to figure out what works and what doesn't. Be careful, though. If you start asking too many questions, you might tip your hand to either a vindictive supervisor or a coworker planning on interviewing for the same position you are. Know who your friends are.

Now is the right time for you to make a friend at the company you are interested in. There is nothing better than inside information. Find someone who is willing to check the internal postings a couple of times a week, or someone who knows someone.

This might be easier than you think. Many companies are now offering finder's fees for technical talent. If an employee submits someone's resume, and the candidate is eventually hired, that employee may have earned a bonus of a few thousand dollars. You would be amazed how many "friends" you'll have if you have the potential of putting a few thousand dollars in their pockets.

(🖐)
recruiter
ⓐdvice

Research a company before going for an interview. Find the company's Web site, or check one of the online stock services if the company is publicly traded. The more information you have going into an interview, the better your chances for having a good interview.

(🖐)
recruiter
ⓐdvice

If you feel that your interviewing skills aren't what they should be, purchase some books, audiocassettes, or videos about interviewing or personal selling. Remember that the purpose of an interview is to sell yourself. You might also try practicing being interviewed with a friend or in front of a mirror.

The Interview

So far, so good. You've been granted an interview. This is no time to forget about your strategy! On the contrary, now is the time to redouble your efforts. This may be your only face-to-face interaction with the company of your dreams. You've got to make a good impression, and you are going to be limited in the amount of time you have to do that.

recruiter advice

If you are going to be more than ten minutes late to an interview, call and ask to speak to the interviewer. Explain the problem, offer an estimated time of arrival, and offer to reschedule the interview. Most recruiters line interviews up back-to-back, so be prepared to reschedule.

Try to ask pointed questions that demonstrate that you know computer systems. For example, you might ask a technical interviewer what WAN protocol is being used. Then you could ask how many redundant routes are available the company is using and whether there is a VPN configuration through the Internet. Ask what applications are being used on the desktop and what bandwidth issues they may present. Find out whether the Y2K issue is presenting any problems.

All of these are great questions if you are talking to a technical interviewer. These are not appropriate questions if you are talking to someone from the human resources department or a senior nontechnical manager. If you're talking to a vice president or a senior manager, don't talk technical, talk business. Ask whether the company has done a Total Cost of Ownership (TCO) analysis, and if so, what the results were. Ask what the acceptable Return on Investment (ROI) is for a capital project.

If you aren't comfortable with these questions, stick to something simpler like asking what projects are in the works for improving productivity, improving reliability, or reducing support costs. These are the issues that business people wrestle with every day. If you want to relate to these folks, you've got to speak their language, and you've got to talk about things that they care about.

recruiter
@dvice

Listen very carefully for the type of question you are being asked in an interview. Answer short-answer questions directly and concisely. Elaborate on open-ended questions. When it's your turn, ask your own mix of direct and open-ended questions.

When answering questions, give direct, concise answers. If you don't know the answer, admit it, then offer your best guess. Guessing is acceptable, as long as you identify your answer as a guess. Don't ever try to pass yourself off as something you are not. A technical interviewer will smell a phony as soon as the answers start to stink.

recruiter
@dvice

When submitting your resume online through electronic mail, use a common file format and a simple font. Avoid any unnecessary graphics. Also, indicate in the e-mail what type of file it is. Your resume should be easy to read.

Working with a Headhunter

As someone looking for a job, I loved working with headhunters. As a recruiter, I hate competing with them. So, for the purpose of this discussion, I'm going to try to think like someone looking for a job.

The really nice thing about headhunters is that most of them are paid a finder's fee that is a percentage of the salary of the person hired. Consequently, the more money you make, the more money your headhunter makes. This is one of the few situations in life in which your agent's best interests are truly your best interests. Also, most headhunters don't get paid at all unless they fill a position. They work fast, and usually with remarkable results.

There are some things to watch out for, though. There are people out there calling themselves career consultants, or even headhunters. They want you to pay them a few hundred dollars to build a resume and to tell you what your ideal job is.

First, you don't need someone to tell you what your ideal job is. You should be able to figure that out on your own. Second, if these people even have a placement service, you would be amazed how many times your ideal job just happens to be the position they are trying to fill. Third, there are too many good recruiters and headhunters out there who don't charge you a dime. You should never, ever pay someone to find you a job! Now give me a second to get off my soapbox...

I guess I get so excited about this topic because I know some really good headhunters who do excellent work. When they make a placement, the company is happy, the employee is happy, and the headhunter made a little money. But there are always a few who give the rest of the recruiting industry a bad name, because they've taken clients' money and left them in the same job, or a worse job.

Headhunters often specialize in a particular type of job, location, or industry. If you are looking for something specific, ask around and find a headhunter who has concentrated on that area. Not only will this person know what is going on in his or her specialty, he or she can help tailor your presentation to that area. That's the real benefit. Think of these specialists as insiders for hire—only you're not paying the bill!

Even if you don't need a specialist, try to narrow down your goals *before* you contact a headhunter. Headhunters aren't in the business of being career counselors. They are in the business of finding you the job you're looking for. That's not to say that they won't help you. On the contrary, they will probably give you a great deal of attention. But only you know what you want.

Put together a professional-looking resume listing every skill you have. Also, put together a cover letter that details what type of job you are looking for, what kind of salary and benefits package you need, and any other interesting bits of information about yourself. This is the documentation that is going to catch the eye of a headhunter.

Your headhunter will then probably take you out to lunch, and you two will have a chat. By the time you're ordering dessert, you will probably have defined your job requirements even more precisely. You may also leave with a list of things to do. The list might include making enhancements to your resume, researching companies, and maybe even scheduling an interview.

On the other hand, the headhunter may tell you point blank that you just aren't qualified for what you want to do, and that there is no way he or she could place you in the job you're looking for. That's hard to hear, but it's probably an honest assessment.

Remember that headhunters only make money if you make money. If a headhunter tells you that you're not qualified, you need to decide whether to continue pursuing this job with another headhunter or look for another job for which you are better suited.

My advice is to swallow your pride, open your mind, and see what the headhunter has to say. Chances are, he or she is going to have some ideas that you might not have considered. At a minimum, you should be able to find out why you aren't qualified and what you need to do to get qualified for the job of your dreams.

One final thought on this topic. A lot of people worry that a headhunter is going to rush them into a job that they won't enjoy, just so the headhunter can get paid. Well, in the first place, you're the decision-maker. Only you can decide whether or not to take a job.

Second, a growing trend in the industry is that a headhunter does not get paid a full commission until the client has held the job for more than six months. I like this trend because, once again, your best interests dovetail with the headhunter's. There's little incentive for a headhunter to put you in a job you're not going to enjoy.

Working with headhunters has been a very positive experience for me. Some of the best jobs I've ever had have come through headhunters. If you find one you like, he or she can be an excellent resource for taking your career where you want it to go.

recruiter @dvice

If you are submitting a resume through an electronic form, use as many keywords as possible. Chances are, the information that you are entering on the form is being entered into a database that will be searched later.

Preparing for the Interview

Start with a little research. You need to be able to talk intelligently about the company you are interviewing with, the industry that company is in, and how you can help this company achieve its goals. At a minimum, you should check out the company's Web site and learn its mission statement, objectives, and goals. You need to demonstrate that you know where this company wants to go and how they are planning to get there.

You can also check out one of the online investment firms to gather information, if the company you're researching is publicly traded. Know what the financial status of the company is. Know whether there are any planned mergers or acquisitions.

You should also try to get a feel for the technology being used in the company. This information could be a little more difficult to obtain than financial information; you may need to find an insider. Be careful of making any recommendations about technology during an interview. After all, you don't want to tell someone how to do his or her job or step on someone's toes. You might, however, be able to identify some troublesome areas that your skills could ease.

Acing the Interview

I wish I could give you a nice, simple formula for ensuring success in an interview. If one exists, I haven't found it, and I don't know anyone who has.

By definition, an interview occurs when two or more people get together for the purpose of filling a job. When you get two people together, there exists the possibility for conflict. Unfortunately, you can do everything right and still have a lousy interview simply because your personality clashed with the personality of the person doing the interviewing.

One of the things that you might consider doing is buying a couple of books, audiotapes, or videos about interviewing or personal selling. There are lots of tapes on how to sell and quite a few about interviewing. All of them will give you some ideas for building a personal relationship with someone in a very short amount of time.

Try to avoid obvious gimmick techniques like commenting on something you see in the person's office. I was on a sales call one time with a junior sales representative who made the mistake of complimenting a manager about the large fish he had mounted on the wall. The manager looked right at the rep and said, "I hate that damn fish. My boss goes on all of these company-sponsored fishing trips, spends a fortune, and then decorates our offices with his stupid fish." The sales call was over before it even began.

This may sound like a cliché, but be yourself. Don't put on airs; don't try to be something you aren't. Most people are not good actors, and most recruiters can spot a performance very quickly. When a recruiter interviews you, he or she wants to get a sense of who you are—not just what you know. Don't make it hard on the recruiters by putting on a show.

When being interviewed, you should appear confident about yourself and your abilities. Practice showing confidence by standing in front of a mirror and "introducing yourself" a few times. Tell your mirror image how happy you are to have an opportunity to interview for the position. Then briefly explain to yourself what your qualifications are and why you would be a good fit for the position. (But avoid telling yourself that you are the *best* candidate for the position. You never know that, and you might be setting yourself up for feeling "robbed" if you're not eventually hired.) Finally, ask yourself a few questions about the job and your own plans, and then answer them. Try this technique. I guarantee it will be the toughest interview you ever have.

Now let's talk for a moment about interview etiquette. I've never seen a formal guide to interview etiquette, but there is certainly an informal set of expectations.

For example, most recruiters are tolerant of a candidate being ten minutes late. Five minutes early is preferable, but ten minutes late is acceptable. Beyond ten minutes, your chances for a successful interview begin to drop precipitously. If you are going to be more than ten minutes late, you definitely need to call, and you can probably expect to reschedule your interview.

Another piece of etiquette involves who speaks first in the interview. Once introductions are made, and everyone is comfortable, the interviewer will ask the first question. That question may be followed by another series of short-answer "warm-up" questions, or the interviewer may ask a more open-ended question.

Open-ended questions are designed to give the person being interviewed an opportunity to talk openly or to bend the conversation toward a topic he or she wants to discuss. Recognize the different types of questions and respond appropriately. If you speak out of turn or fail to answer appropriately, you are running the risk of annoying the interviewer and having your interview cut short.

Incidentally, if the interviewer asks you a trick question, and it's obvious that it is a trick question, call him or her on it. Let him or her know that you're not afraid to call a donkey a donkey. Most interviewers will appreciate this and probably accord you a little more respect as a result.

(✋)
**recruiter
advice**

Be yourself in an interview. Most recruiters can spot a phony or an actor in just a few minutes. You need to be open and honest about who you are, what you can do, and what you want in return. Don't make the interviewer pry this information out of you.

Following Up on the Interview

Always follow up on an interview. This can be done with a simple thank-you card or phone call.

You're trying to accomplish several things with the follow-up: refreshing the memories of the decision makers (who may have interviewed numerous candidates), projecting a positive impression, and demonstrating interest and eagerness to work for this company.

Don't worry about looking desperate; you are more likely to come off as confident and professional. Never worry about following up an interview with a phone call to check the status of your application. In many companies, the people doing the interviewing are also the people doing real work. Interviewing is not their primary responsibility. Consequently, applications sometimes slip through the cracks. It may be up to you to keep the ball rolling by continuing to call and ask questions. You might get hired through persistence alone.

(✋)
**recruiter
advice**

Always follow up on an interview with a phone call or a thank-you card. You want an interviewer to be reminded of you after the interview is over. You might be just one applicant in hundreds, so you have to find ways of making yourself stand out.

(✋)
**recruiter
advice**

Never stop looking for your perfect job. You should test the waters and go out on an interview or talk to a headhunter once every six months. High-tech industries change rapidly, and with that change comes a myriad of new opportunities.

4

Software Guide

The *Personal Testing Center* is easy to install on any Windows 95/98/NT computer. Just double-click the Setup file on the CD and the installation will begin. With the *Personal Testing Center,* you are given the option to run the programs directly from the CD or to install them to your hard drive.

Installing the CCNA Test Yourself Personal Testing Center

Double-clicking on Setup will cycle you through two introductory pages on the *Test Yourself* software. On the third page, you will have to read and accept the license agreement. Once you have read the agreement, click on the Next button and you will be brought to the *Personal Testing Center's* main page. Here you will have the option to run the exams directly or to install them to your hard drive.

Installing the *Personal Testing Center* to your hard drive is an easy process. Click on the Install to Hard Drive icon, and the procedure will start for you. An instructional box will appear and will walk you through the remainder of the installation. If installed on the hard drive, the *Personal Testing Center* program group will be created in the Start Programs folder.

Should you wish to run the software from the CD-ROM, the steps are the same until you reach the point where you would select the Install to Hard Drive icon. Here, select the Run from CD icon, and the exam will automatically begin.

To uninstall the program from your hard disk, use the add/remove programs feature in your Windows Control panel. InstallShield will run uninstall.

Test Type Choices

With the *Personal Testing Center,* you have three options in which to run the program: Live, Practice, and Review. Each test type will draw from a pool of over 2,000 potential questions. Choosing between the different test types will depend on whether you would like to simulate an actual Cisco exam, receive instant feedback on your answer choices, or use the testing simulator to review concepts. The following sections will discuss the differences between each of the testing formats and the recommended usage for each format for learning the material presented. Figure 4-1 shows the screen on which the various modes of test operation are shown. Note that selecting the Full Screen icon on Internet Explorer's Standard toolbar gives you the best display of the *Personal Testing Center.*

FIGURE 4-1   The *Personal Testing Center's* test type choices

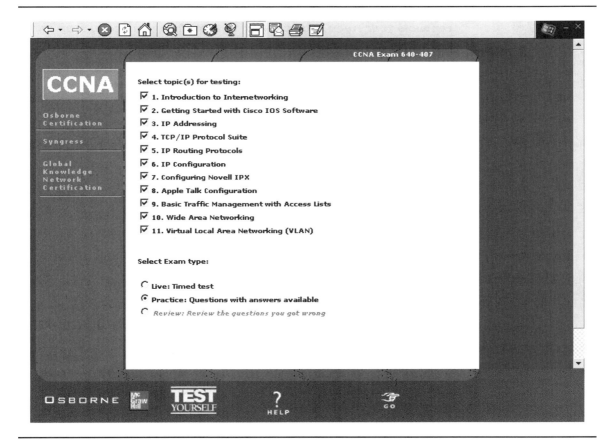

Live

The Live timed test type is meant to reflect the actual Cisco exam as closely as possible. You will have 60 minutes in which to complete the exam. You will have the option to skip questions and return to them later, move to the previous question, or end the exam. Once the timer has expired, you will automatically go to the scoring page to review your test results.

I strongly recommend that you complete the Live exam and review your score, but do not review the correct answers. Once you review the correct answers, you will be more likely to memorize answers, not the material being presented. If the postexam summary screen determines you are below passing in a certain area, you should then redouble your study in that area and take the exam again. Even on the second try, do not review the correct answers.

Practice

When choosing the Practice exam type, you have the option of receiving instant feedback as to whether your selected answer is correct. The questions will be presented to you in numerical order and will contain every question in the available question pool for each section you chose to be tested on.

As with the Live exam type, you have the option of continuing through the entire exam without seeing the correct answer for each question. The number of questions you answered correctly, along with the percentage of correct answers, will be displayed during the postexam summary report. Once you have selected what you believe is the correct answer(s), click the Review Answer icon to display the correct answer.

You should review the correct answers only after you have completed the Live exam a few times without looking at the answers. Take your time and make sure you understand why each answer is correct, as well as the thought process involved in reaching the correct answer. If you do not completely understand the material presented in the question, you should review the corresponding material in one of the approved study guides.

You have the option of ending the practice exam at any time, but your postexam summary screen may reflect an incorrect percentage, based on the number of questions you failed to answer. Questions that are skipped are counted as incorrect answers on the postexam summary screen.

Review

During the Review exam type, you will be presented with questions similar to both the Live and Practice exam types. The Review Answer icon, however, is not present, since every question will have the correct answer posted near the bottom of the screen, as shown in Figure 4-2. You have the

FIGURE 4-2 Review mode shows the correct answer at the bottom of the screen

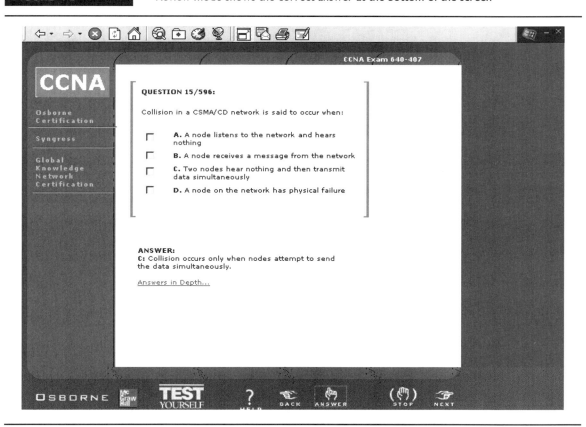

option of answering the question without looking at the correct answer. In the Review exam type, you can also return to previous questions and skip to the next question, as well as end the exam by clicking the End the Exam icon.

The Review exam type is recommended when you have already completed the Live exam type once or twice, and would now like to determine which answers you in fact got correct.

Questions with Answers

For the Practice and Review exam type you will have the option of clicking a hyperlink titled Answers in Depth, which will present relevant study material aimed at exposing the logic behind the answer in a separate browser window.

By having two browsers open (one for the test engine and one for the review information) you can quickly alternate between the two windows while keeping your place in the exam. You will find that additional windows are not generated as you follow hyperlinks throughout the test engine. Figure 4-3 shows an example of this set up.

Test Topics

The *CCNA Test Yourself Personal Testing Center* sections are organized around the objectives Cisco has established for the 640-407 exam. For further review, we recommend the companion *Cisco Certified Network Associate Study Guide* from Global Knowledge Certification Press. The chapters in these books correspond directly to the sections of the exams.

Scoring

The *CCNA Test Yourself Personal Testing Center* postexam summary screen, called Benchmark Yourself, displays the results for each section you chose to be tested on, including a bar graph similar to the real exam, which displays the percentage of correct answers. You can compare your percentage to the

FIGURE 4-3 Running two browser windows, one with the live test and one with the review information

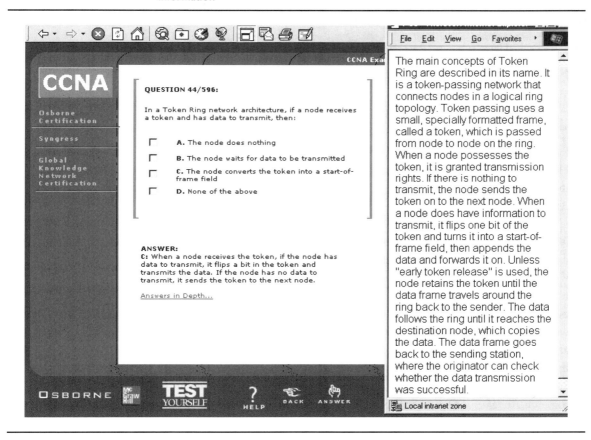

actual passing percentage for each section. The percentage displayed on the postexam summary screen is not the actual percentage required to pass the exam. You'll see the number of questions you answered correctly compared to the total number of questions you were tested on. If you choose to skip a question, it will be marked as incorrect. Ending the exam by clicking the End button with questions still unanswered lowers your percentage, as these questions will be marked as incorrect.

FROM THE CLASSROOM

Personal Testing Center FAQs
Managing Browser Windows

The testing application runs inside an Internet Explorer 4.0 browser window. We recommend that you use the full-screen view to minimize the amount of text scrolling you need to do. However, the application will initiate a second iteration of the browser when you link to an Answer in Depth or a Review Graphic. If you are running in full-screen view, the second iteration of the browser will be covered by the first. You can toggle between the two windows with ALT-TAB, you can click your taskbar to maximize the second window, or you can get out of full-screen mode and arrange the two windows so they are both visible on the screen at the same time. The application will not initiate more than two browser windows, so you aren't left with hundreds of open windows for each Answer in Depth or Review Graphic that you view.

Saving Scores as Cookies

Your exam score is stored as a browser cookie. If you've configured your browser to accept cookies, your score will be stored in a cookie named History. If you don't accept cookies, you cannot permanently save your scores. If you delete the History cookie, the scores will be deleted permanently.

Using the Browser Buttons

The test application runs inside the Internet Explorer 4.0 browser. You should navigate from screen to screen by using the application's buttons, not the browser's buttons.

JavaScript Errors

If you encounter a JavaScript error, you should be able to proceed within the application. If you cannot, shut down your Internet Explorer 4.0 browser session and relaunch the testing application.

exam
Watch

Scores for the Benchmark Yourself feature are stored in IE4 as a cookie named History. If you delete this cookie, you will delete your score history.

Clicking the End button and then the Home button allows you to choose another exam type or test yourself on another section. Figure 4-4 illustrates the scoring section of the test program.

FIGURE 4-4   Getting a score

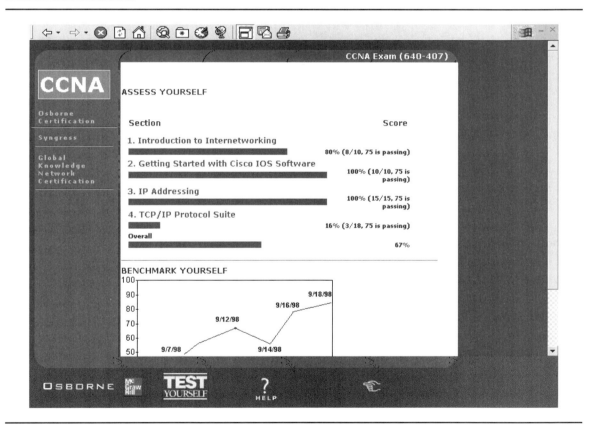

5

The CCNA Most Wanted List

Everyone can use a little help when it comes to passing these challenging Cisco examinations. Having the most study resources at your fingertips, whether it be an approved study guide, Web page, or testing software, will increase your chances of passing the exams. Not only do these resources prove invaluable when it comes to becoming certified, you can use these resources in the real world when you are faced with a challenging network problem and need to do some research. After all, no one has all the answers: but you should at least know where to begin looking for information.

A good phrase to remember is "Repetition is the mother of skill." What this means is that the more often you repeat something, the more competent you become. Let's face it, studying the same thing over and over can become mind-numbing. But a few weeks or months after being certified on the CCNA test, you may find that a refresher will only sharpen your abilities and may even pay off in the workplace.

Another time that reviewing the CCNA materials will come in handy is at the beginning of a new network project. Every new project presents an element of the unknown. How is the network designed? What problems are being experienced on it? What protocols are being used? What would be the optimal network performance? How much growth is being experienced? And how can you fix the problems that exist now and prevent the ones that will happen in the future? Once in a while—well, almost always—the answer to this last question is found in materials you have at your fingertips.

Resources for Studying

There are a number of resources to help you in your quest to become a CCNA, from Internet sites to books and self-test software. The trick is to find the right amount of material to ensure you'll pass the exam without spending a fortune in the process. Most CCNAs with whom I have talked agree that you should have two books for each exam, self-test software, and help from several of the Internet Cisco Web sites. You should begin by reading the books once or twice, and by using the Cisco exam objectives to determine the material that will be on the exam. Using the Internet Cisco Web sites can refine your areas of study to concepts that other test takers have found vital to passing the exam. And, finally, self-test software can simulate the testing center experience and help you monitor your progress, determine weak areas, and master key concepts.

Online Sites

Probably the best site I have found on the Internet for corresponding with others who have taken these certification tests is http://www.CCIEPrep.com, in the Talk CCIE or Talk CCNA section of the Web site. You will find here not only postings from people who are studying for the test like yourself, but from "veterans" who share their test-taking experiences with the rest of the group. I visited this site while I was studying, and I found it kept me on the right track, focusing on what is really important for the exam.

In addition to the forums, this site offers online information that contains test-taking hints, suggestions, and articles relating to the exam you are preparing for. These are professional articles by certified trainers and engineers who have been through the experiences you are going through.

The second site that I would recommend is http://www.groupstudy.com. It is a companion site for a Cisco mailing list. As a companion, it contains archives of information that are invaluable for a CCNA candidate.

The Cisco Mailing List

When I took the CCNA exams, a very helpful resource for determining what the exam would cover in terms of connectivity was the Cisco Groupstudy mailing list. You can subscribe to this list and receive e-mail that is similar to a forum discussion, but the information is compiled and sent to you every day. While you are reading through the various posts and brain dumps on exams, you can compile your own text file for each exam you are preparing to take. Copy important test hints and paste them into your exam-specific document. After a couple weeks, you can create quite a large document of what to expect on the exam. If you know you are going to take an exam a few months down the road, begin by compiling your document now, and you'll have an invaluable resource later.

To subscribe to the CCNA mailing list, send an e-mail message to listserver@groupstudy.com with the following in the message:

SUBSCRIBE CISCO

A Cisco mailing list is available for discussions of real-world technical issues. Discussions about Cisco hardware operation, problems, features, topology, configuration, protocols, routing, loading, and serving are all encouraged. To join the list, an e-mail should be sent to

cisco-request@spot.colorado.edu

CCNA Mailing List Archives

If you are just now subscribing to the Cisco or the Groupstudy mailing list, you have already missed some very valuable exam information. But don't despair; you can visit the gigantic vault of information in the mailing list archives. Go to http://www.groupstudy.com/ to see hundreds of messages from users. The Cisco mailing list archives are available via anonymous FTP from spot.Colorado.EDU in the subdirectory cisco.

Once the page has finished loading, you may have to use your Web browser's Find feature to search for relevant topics in the subject line, such as TCP/IP. Once you get some hits, you can bring up the message and read the post.

Global Knowledge Certification Press Study Guides

The Global Knowledge Certification Press Study Guides, from Osborne/McGraw-Hill, offer thorough coverage of their subject areas, presented in such a way as to help you prepare for the corresponding Cisco exams. In both book and CD-ROM formats, you will find an abundance of practice questions, exercises, quick chapter summaries, and tips about proven techniques of exam-taking success. In a special feature, "From the Classroom," a Cisco instructor reviews important information about problem areas for students and offers advice on how to avoid common pitfalls.

The following table gives a brief summary of the wealth of information you'll find in each Cisco study guide.

CCNA Study Guide	Apply the OSI Protocol Reference model to networking components. Understand the various layers of the OSI model and how they manage network traffic. Configure a Cisco switch and hub. Select the appropriate mode to make configuration changes on a Cisco router. Learn to navigate the Cisco IOS. Select and use the appropriate IP addresses, masks, and subnets. Select and use the appropriate routing protocol. Configure TCP/IP, IPX, AppleTalk, and WAN protocols. Manage traffic using access lists. Understand and configure VLANs.
Cisco Advanced Cisco Router Configuration Study Guide	Make a network scalable. Manage TCP/IP, IPX, and AppleTalk traffic. Configure router queues. Configure and load balance IGRP routers. Configure and verify OSPF and NLSP routing. Understand EIGRP and configure it on a Cisco router. Understand and configure BGP. Configure WAN protocols such as Frame Relay. Configure bridging protocols on a router. Understand and configure DLSW+.
Cisco Internetwork Troubleshooting Study Guide	Apply the generic problem-solving model. Review LAN protocol responsibilities and how they are applied in an internetwork. Troubleshoot WAN connections. Review TCP/IP protocols, their ports, and how they are used. Understand common end-user tasks and what happens behind the scenes. Review IPX protocol stack and routing. Understand how printing really works. Apply knowledge of common user tasks to AppleTalk. Explain the difference between broadcast, multicast, and directed network traffic. Review routing protocol behavior. Use router diagnostic tools, including CiscoWorks and third-party tools.

Don't let the real test be your first test! These Cisco certification study guides are geared to help you pass the various exams. Curriculum based, classroom proven, and completely up-to-date, these official Global Knowledge books are your key to becoming Cisco certified. These guides have self-test questions, study drills, real-life tips, and exam preparation hints. Special features include

- **Exam Watch** Warnings based on thorough postexam research identifying the most troublesome exam questions—and how to answer them correctly!

- **From the Classroom** Discussions of important issues direct from Global Knowledge's award-winning instructors

- **Certification Exercises** Step-by-step exercises that focus on specific skills most likely to be on the exam

- **Two-Minute Drill** Quick and concise checklists that summarize a chapter's main points—perfect for last-minute review!

- **Chapter Self Tests** Chapter-specific questions similar to those found on the exam, geared to reinforce your learning experience

- **How to Take the Exam** Key pointers on how to maximize your chances for success on exam day

- **Free Membership** To Global Knowledge's Access Global Web site—exam updates, assessment tools, and tips for success

Part II

Excerpts from Cisco Certified Network Associate Study Guide (Exam 640-407)

The following three chapters are excerpted directly from the third printing of the best-selling *CCNA Cisco Certified Network Associate Study Guide*. These chapters will help you review the basic internetworking information needed to pass the CCNA exam. The full-size study guide/CD-ROM, available in traditional and online bookstores, contains 11 chapters and covers all the newest official Cisco CCNA exam objectives.

1

Introduction to Internetworking

Cisco Certified Internetworking Engineers, or CCIEs, are recognized as some of the premiere internetworking professionals in the information systems industry. Their understanding of the intricacies of internetwork design and architecture stems from both dedicated study and experience. To attain the highest level of certification—the CCIE—one is required to be able to

- Design new internetworks
- Document existing internetworks
- Locate the cause of internetwork problems
- Resolve bottlenecks
- Redesign existing internetworks
- Understand and be able to connect internetworks to the Internet
- Configure new Cisco routers, switches, and hubs
- Reconfigure existing Cisco routers, switches, and hubs
- Understand Cisco Internetworking Operating System software
- Upgrade and repair Cisco routers, switches, and hubs

To start you on your certification path, this book provides you with the information needed to become a Cisco Certified Network Associate (CCNA). A potential CCNA must have the knowledge to install, configure, and operate simple-routed LAN, routed WAN, and switched LAN and LANE networks.

This is the beginning of an adventure in knowledge. What this book can offer as both a reference and a learning tool can take an engineer to the heights of an internetworking career.

CERTIFICATION OBJECTIVE 1.01

The Internetworking Model

There is a distinction made between networking and internetworking. Networking is the process and methodology applied to connecting multiple computers so that they are able to exchange information. Internetworking is the process and methodology applied to connecting multiple networks, regardless of their physical topologies and distance. Internetworking has evolved with the rapid growth and change in networking. Because of this, the basic building blocks and reference models for networking are also used and applied to internetworking.

Network Evolution

Internetworks evolved from necessity. In the early days of computing (the 1950s and 1960s), internetworks did not exist. Computers were autonomous and proprietary. In the late 1960s, however, the United States Department of Defense (DOD), became interested in academic research being done on a packet-switched wide area network design. "Packet" referred to a small bundle of data. "Switched" referred to the use of a routing system similar to the switch-based telephone system. And "wide area network" (WAN) meant that the network would extend over sites that were physically distant from each other.

DOD wanted to use this technology for national defense, as a means to share radar data, and distribute control and commands in the case of a nuclear war. The agency within DOD that handled the network research was the Advanced Research Projects Agency (ARPA), which later prefixed "Defense" to the beginning of their name and became known as DARPA. The DARPA project included scientists and engineers from universities and the Bolt, Baranek and Newman company of Massachusetts, who faced the two challenges in this project: *interconnectivity* and *interoperability*.

- **Interconnectivity**   The means of transporting information between the computers, inclusive of the physical media, the data packaging mechanism, and the routing between multiple network equipment pieces from the starting node until reaching the destination node.

- **Interoperability**   The methodology applied to make data understandable to computers that use proprietary or simply different computer operating systems and languages.

The result of the DARPA project was ARPANET, which eventually became the Internet, and the evolution of the IP protocol suite, which was then included as part of Berkeley's version of UNIX. ARPANET grew into the Internet by including networks in other government and university campuses. That grew even further with the inclusion of commercial enterprise networks.

Networks did not become prevalent in corporations until the 1980s when the personal computer (PC) became popular. After companies realized that sharing hard disk space on some of the earliest file servers enabled employees to share data easily and further boosted productivity, they implemented networks on a large scale. They created LANs (Local Area Networks) and then connected them into WANs (Wide Area Networks). After the Internet went commercial in the early 1990s, corporations began to connect to it as well.

The OSI Model

There are two standards to consider in internetworking: *de jure*, and *de facto*. De jure means by right or legal establishment. De facto means established by actual fact, though not officially or legally recognized. The evolution of TCP/IP created a de facto standard for that protocol, because it grew and became accepted, although it was not proposed as a standard until after its wide acceptance. The OSI (Open System Interconnection) reference model is a de jure standard.

The International Organization for Standardization (ISO) created the OSI model and released it in 1984 in order to provide a network model for vendors such that their products would interoperate on networks. The OSI reference model provides a hierarchical tool for understanding networking technology, as well as a basis for current and future network developments.

This model also takes into account the interconnectivity and interoperability challenges faced by the DARPA project engineers. The way that the OSI model answered these challenges was through a seven-layer protocol suite model, illustrated in Figure 1-1. By dividing the model into layers, the capability to interoperate and interconnect became manageable, since each layer was self-contained, not relying on the operating system or other factors. The layered approach benefited vendors, too, since they only needed to concentrate development efforts on the layers that their own product used, and could rely on the existing protocols at other layers. Not

FIGURE 1-1

OSI reference model

Layer 7 - Provides services directly to applications
The applications can vary, but includes electronic
messaging.

| Application |

Layer 6 - Formats data in order to provide a
common interface for applications. This can
include encryption services

| Presentation |

Layer 5 - Establishes end connections between two
nodes. Services include establishing whether a
connection can be set at full or half duplex-although
duplex is actually handled at layer 4.

| Session |

Layer 4 - General data delivery-connection-oriented
or connectionless. Includes full or half duplex, flow
control and error recovery services.

| Transport |

Layer 3 - This layer establishes the connection
between two nodes through addressing. It includes
routing and relaying of data through an
internetwork.

| Network |

Layer 2 - Frames data and handles flow control at
this layer. This layer specifies the topology and
provides hardware addressing.

| Data link |

Layer 1 - Transmission of the raw bit stream,
electrical signaling, and hardware interface.

| Physical |

only are development costs kept to a minimum, but marketability is
increased, since the product works with other vendors' products.

The model describes how each layer communicates with a corresponding
layer on the other node. Figure 1-2 illustrates how data works its way
through a network. At the first node, the end user creates some data to be
sent to the other node, such as an e-mail. At the application layer, an
application header is added to the data. The presentation layer adds its own
header to the data received from the application layer. Each layer adds its

own header to the data received from the layer above. However, at lower layers, the data is broken up into smaller units and headers added to each of the units. For instance, the transport layer will have smaller datagrams, the network layer will have packets, and the data link layer will have frames. The physical layer handles the data in a raw bitstream. When this bitstream is received at the destination, the data is reassembled at each layer, and the headers of each layer discarded, until the e-mail is readable by the end user.

FIGURE 1-2   How the OSI model transports data

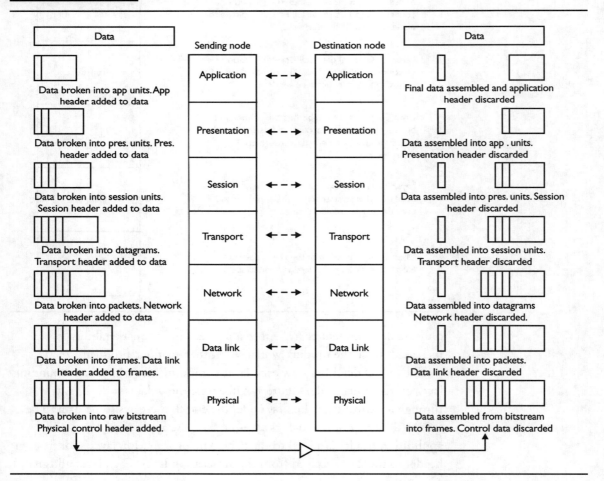

A common mnemonic device for remembering the layers (application, presentation, session, transport, network, data link, physical) in the right order is **A**ll **P**eople **S**eem **T**o **N**eed **D**ata **P**rocessing.

Encapsulation

Encapsulation is the process of adding a header to the data, or *wrapping* the data. In order to send data out on a Token Ring network, the data must be wrapped with the Token Ring header before it is transmitted. The terms wrapping and encapsulation refer to both the header and the ending bits that are added to each bundle of data. Header bits are used to signify the beginning of a data bundle, and frequently include addressing and other features, depending on the protocol and layer. The ending bits are typically used for error checking. Header bits receive more attention, since they include most of the protocol feature implementation.

Encapsulation may occur at each layer in the OSI reference model. The entire packet from each layer is inserted into the data field of the next layer, and another header is added. Occasionally a layer splits the data unit (including previous layer header) into multiple, smaller data units, and each one of the smaller units is wrapped with a new header from the lower protocol layer. This process helps control data flow and addresses packet size limitations on the network. As the data moves down the model, it becomes smaller and more uniform in size and content.

When data is received, the corresponding layer at the receiving node reassembles the data field before passing it to the next layer. As the data moves back up the model at the destination, it is pieced back together like a puzzle.

CERTIFICATION OBJECTIVE 1.02

Physical and Data Link Layers

The physical layer, or layer 1, defines the actual mechanical specifications and electrical data bitstream. This includes the voltage level, the voltage changes, and the definition of which voltage level is a 1 and which is a 0.

The data rate of transmission, the maximum distances, and even physical connectors are all included in this level.

The data link layer, or layer 2, is also known as the link layer. It consists of two sublayers, the upper level being the Logical Link Control (LLC), and the lower level being the Media Access Control (MAC). Hardware addresses are actually MAC addresses in the data link layer. The physical address is placed here, since the physical layer handles only raw bitstream functions. The data is broken into small "frames" at this layer.

The physical and data link layers are usually implemented together in hardware/software combination solutions. Examples include hubs, switches and network adapters, and their applicable software drivers, as well as the media or cables used to connect the network nodes. The remaining layers are usually implemented in software only.

The IEEE (Institute for Electrical and Electronics Engineers) created several standards under the 802 series. Table 1-1 describes the 802 series of standards that are currently in existence or are still being developed.

TABLE 1-1	Standard	Description
IEEE 802 Standards Series	802.2	Defines LLC protocol that other 802 standards can use
	802.3	Ethernet (CSMA/CD)
	802.3u	Fast Ethernet 100BaseT
	802.4	Token Bus (rarely used)
	802.5	Token Ring
	802.6	MANs (Metropolitan Area Network) using two fiber-optic buses in opposing directions
	802.9	Isochronous Ethernet – channel sharing between one async channel and 96 dedicated channels providing 16 Mbps
	802.11	Wireless LANs using CSMA/CA (Carrier Sense Multiple Access/Collision Avoidance)
	802.12	100VG-AnyLAN

DIX and 802.3 Ethernet

Digital, Intel, and Xerox (collectively known as DIX) created Ethernet in the 1970s. This was used as the basis for the IEEE 802.3 standard released in 1980. DIX then updated their standard to match the IEEE 802.3 version. The term Ethernet is commonly used to refer to either one of these network standards.

However, Ethernet and IEEE 802.3 do have some differences. One difference is that 802.3 specifies the physical layer and the MAC portion of the data link layer, while DIX Ethernet specifies the entire physical and data link layers. 802.3 specifies different physical layers, but DIX Ethernet only specifies one. Table 1-2 compares the two standards.

Ethernet uses a carrier sense multiple access/collision detection (CSMA/CD) method. In the CSMA/CD network, nodes can access the network any time they have data to send. Before a node transmits data, it "listens" to see if the network is busy. If not, the node transmits data. If the network is in use, the node waits. Collisions occur if two nodes listen, hear nothing and then access the wire simultaneously. This ruins both transmissions, and both stations have to try a second time. There is a *backoff algorithm* that creates a random wait time for retransmissions so that a second collision will not occur. Figure 1-3 illustrates this process.

Ethernet, including 802.3, is a *broadcast* system. That means that all nodes see all data frames, whether or not that data is meant to be received

TABLE 1-2		Physical Layer Specifications for IEEE 802.3 and DIX Ethernet					
	DIX	**IEEE 802.3 Physical Standards**					
	Ethernet	10BaseF	1Base5	10Broad36	10Base2	10Base5	10BaseT
Rate Mbps	10	10	1	10	10	10	10
Topology	Bus	Star	Star	Bus	Bus	Bus	Star
Media	50-ohm thick coaxial	Fiber-optic cable	Unshielded twisted-pair	75-ohm coaxial	50-ohm thin coaxial	50-ohm thick coaxial	Unshielded twisted-pair

Collisions on CSMA/CD
network

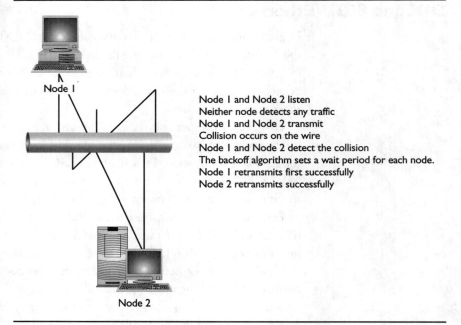

Node 1

Node 1 and Node 2 listen
Neither node detects any traffic
Node 1 and Node 2 transmit
Collision occurs on the wire
Node 1 and Node 2 detect the collision
The backoff algorithm sets a wait period for each node.
Node 1 retransmits first successfully
Node 2 retransmits successfully

Node 2

by that node. Each node examines the frame header addresses as the frames
are received to determine if they are destined for that node. If not, the
frames are forwarded on the network. If they are destined for the node, it
passes them to the upper-level protocols for processing.

The IEEE 802.3 frame, shown in Figure 1-4, begins with a *preamble* of
alternating 1's and 0's that tells the receiving station that this is a new frame.
The next byte is a start-of-frame delimiter (SOF) that ends with two
consecutive one bits. The next part of the frame header is the destination and
source address fields. An address consists of three bytes identifying the vendor,
and a second three bytes that are specified by the vendor. After the source
address, in IEEE 802.3 frames, there is a two-byte field that discloses the
number of bytes of data contained within the frame. The data itself is next, at
a minimum of 64 bytes (padded with extra bytes if it is too short), and finally
the four-byte FCS field (Frame Check Sequence) ends the frame. The FCS
field includes a cyclic redundancy check (CRC) value that is used to check for
damage that may have happened to the data during transmission.

FIGURE 1-4

IEEE 802.3 frame format

Preamble	SOF	Destination address	Source address	Length field	Data	FCS

802.5 Token Ring

Token Ring networks were originally a proprietary network specification created by IBM in the 1970s. Token Ring networks are nearly identical and compatible with the IEEE 802.5 specification developed later, which was based on IBM's Token Ring. The differences include

- IEEE 802.5 does not specify a physical topology, but IBM's Token Ring specifies a star topology using a multistation access unit.

- IEEE 802.5 does not specify a medium, but IBM's Token Ring specifies twisted-pair wiring.

The main concepts of Token Ring are described in its name. It is a token-passing network that connects nodes in a logical ring topology. Token passing (illustrated in Figure 1-5) uses a small, specially formatted frame, called a token, which is passed from node to node on the ring. When a node possesses the token, it is granted transmission rights. If there is nothing to transmit, the node sends the token on to the next node. When a node does have information to transmit, it flips one bit of the token and turns it into a start-of-frame field, then appends the data and forwards it on. Unless "early token release" is used, the node retains the token until the data frame travels around the ring back to the sender. The data follows the ring until it reaches the destination node, which copies the data. The data frame goes back to the sending station, where the originator can check whether the data transmission was successful.

There is also a method for *token seizing*, (or *access priority*) in Token Ring, whereby priority can be assigned to stations so that they can use the network more frequently. A station with equal or higher priority than the priority value contained in a token can seize it for its use. In doing so, it raises the token's priority, and returns it to the original priority on the next pass.

FIGURE 1-5	Token passing

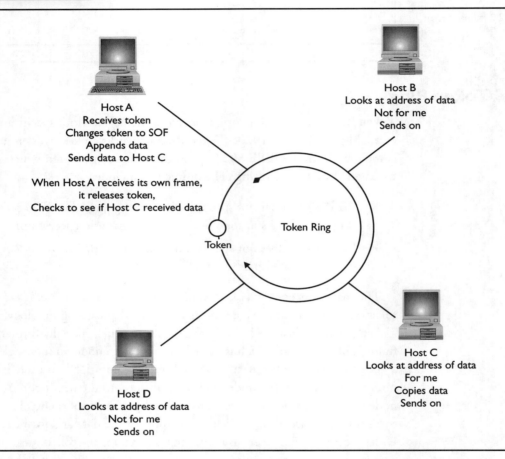

Beaconing is a Token Ring mechanism that detects network faults. If a station detects a failure in the network, it sends a beacon frame, which specifies the reporting station, its nearest active upstream neighbor (NAUN), and the failure area. Beaconing triggers *autoreconfiguration*, in which the network nodes attempt to reconfigure the network around the failed areas. A multistation access unit (MSAU) may "wrap" a port so that it is not part of the ring, bypassing all inactive or nonfunctional ports, but including all active, functioning ones.

There are two types of frames, a token and a data frame. A token (shown in Figure 1-6) is three bytes long. A data frame (shown in Figure 1-7) consists of the data sent by upper-layer protocols and the Token Ring header. There is a special data frame called a MAC frame, for commands that consist of Token Ring control information and header.

ANSI FDDI

In the mid 1980s, ANSI (American National Standards Institute) X3T9.5 standards committee created FDDI (Fiber Distributed Data Interface), which was developed to address the growing bandwidth needs in network systems. ANSI submitted FDDI to the International Organization for Standardization, which then created a compatible FDDI standard. The FDDI standard specifies the physical and MAC portion of the data link layers for a token-passing, dual-ring topology using fiber-optic media at 100 Mbps. Fiber has some advantages over copper wire:

- Immunity to electrical interference
- Higher throughput
- Immunity to traditional wiretap methods
- Capacity to be used for longer distances

The MAC layer specification defines the media access method, frame format, token passing method, MAC addressing, CRC (cyclic redundancy

---

FIGURE 1-6

Token Ring token format

Contains priority
and reservation
fields. Also contains the
token bit.

| Start delimiter | Access control | End delimiter |

Alerts stations of a
coming token

Notifies that this is
the end of the frame

Contains
information for
verifying the
frame's accuracy

check), and error recovery. The physical layer specification defines the data
framing, clocking requirements, and transmission media (bit error rates,
optical components, fiber-optic connector, power levels). Also, FDDI
provides for the station configuration, insertion, removal, fault recovery,
ring configuration, and control.

In the dual ring configuration, traffic travels in one direction on one
ring, and the other direction on the other ring. One ring is primary, and
used for data transmission. The other is secondary, and used for backup.
Class B stations attach to a single ring through a concentrator so that
rebooting a station will not bring down the ring. Class B stations are known
as SAS (single-attached stations). Class A stations attach to both rings, and
are known as DAS (dual-attached stations). The dual ring provides fault
tolerance, as shown in Figure 1-8. If a Class A station on the dual ring fails,
it creates a ring failure. During that failure, stations on either side of the
fault wrap their ports, restoring service through the backup ring. If there is
more than one break in the ring, multiple separate rings can be the result.

FDDI supports both asynchronous and synchronous traffic.
Synchronous is allocated a portion of the bandwidth for stations requiring
continuous transmission; asynchronous is allocated the remainder. Stations
using the asynchronous portion are assigned priority from a priority scheme
of eight levels, which are shown in Figure 1-9.

MAC Addresses

The data link layer consists of two sublayers: Logical Link Control (LLC)
and Media Access Control (MAC). The MAC sublayer determines the
address for the hardware at that layer. This address is network independent,
such that wherever the hardware is "plugged in" to the internetwork, it
would have the same MAC address, regardless of the network address. The
vendor usually assigns the MAC address. In the Ethernet scheme, a series of

Dual ring fault tolerance

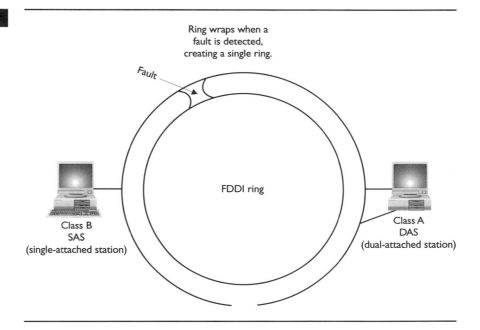

Ethernet MAC addresses are assigned to a vendor, who then assigns a different address to each interface produced. An Ethernet MAC address consists of 12 digits. The first six digits (the Organizationally Unique Identifier, or OUI) are the unique number assigned to the vendor by the IEEE, and the remaining six digits are the series. As a result, each network interface card will have a different MAC address on any given LAN or WAN.

Interfaces

The physical layer encompasses several different types of interfaces. These are either dictated by the protocol used on the segment, or by the proprietary specification of the vendor. Interfaces are used to connect data terminal

FDDI frame format

Preamble	Start delimiter	Frame control	Destination address	Source address	Data	End delimiter	Frame status

equipment (DTE) and data circuit-terminating equipment (DCE) devices. DTEs are network nodes such as routers and servers. DCEs are internetworking devices, such as packet switches, generally owned by the carrier, which provide clocking and switching.

RS-232

RS-232 is the EIA (Electronics Industries Alliance) serial port interface standard. In the RS-232 serial port, one pin is used to transmit data, another to receive data. The remaining pins are used to establish and maintain communication between two serial devices. There is both a 25-pin (DB-25) and a 9-pin (DB-9) version. The cable media must be configured so that each wire transmits or receives the type of data expected. RS-232 cables, which are rated to 19.2 Kbps, must be configured to properly connect DCE and DTE devices. Unique pinouts are required for cables that do not conform to the standard. The pinouts are described in Table 1-3.

V.35

ITU-T (International Telecommunication Union—Telecommunication Standardization Sector) created an entire V.*xx* series of standards. The V.35 standard is a physical layer protocol suitable for connections to a packet network at speeds up to 48 Kbps, and beyond, even to 4 Mbps. This standard specifies synchronous communication.

HSSI

Both the ISO and the ITU-T are currently reviewing HSSI (High Speed Serial Interface) for standardization. HSSI is a DTE/DCE interface that handles high-speed communication over WAN links. This is a physical layer specification of a point-to-point connection that runs at speeds up to 52 Mbps using shielded twisted-pair copper wire.

BRI Interfaces

BRI (Basic Rate Interface) is an ISDN (Integrated Services Digital Network) term for an ISDN connection consisting of two B channels at 64 Kbps and one D channel at 16 Kbps. A terminal adapter is a modem-like

TABLE 1-3		RS-232 Pinouts		
9 Pin	**25 Pin**	**Symbol**	**Signal Sent on That Pin**	**Input/Output Data**
-	1		Protective ground	
3	2	TX	Transmit data	Output
2	3	RX	Receive data	Input
7	4	RTS	Request to send	Output
8	5	CTS	Clear to send	Input
6	6	DSR	Data set ready	Input
5	7		Signal ground	
1	8	DCD	Data carrier detect	Input
-	9		Transmit current loop +	Output
-	11		Transmit current loop -	Output
-	18		Receive current loop +	Input
4	20	DTR	Data terminal ready	Output
9	22	RI	Ring indicator	Input
-	23		Data signal rate indicator	Input and Output
-	25		Receive current loop -	Input

device used to connect the DTE device to the ISDN circuit. The ITU-T's BRI standard specification for the physical layer includes data transmission for the B channels and signaling, framing control, and other overhead control information on the D channel.

Network Clock

Synchronizing network timing is handled at the physical layer of the OSI reference model. This clocking of the network bitstream can improve throughput, and is mandatory for WAN circuits. Specifications for clocking are included in the framing format and control mechanisms defined in interface standards.

FROM THE CLASSROOM

Setting Up a Lab Network

This is a long chapter, filled with dry information about abstract concepts. In the ICRC classes, this material used to take the better part of the first day. The students were always frustrated, because their primary motivation in coming to class in the first place was to get their hands on some actual routers! One of the things we used to do to help break up the tedium of non-stop lectures was to have the students help cable up the classroom network. In contrast to the course's focus on layer 3, with a little about layer 2, putting the equipment together into a network is purely a physical layer activity. I'd like to walk you through some of the considerations for setting up a classroom or a lab network, in case you need to set up one of your own someday.

The classroom network uses a combination of Ethernet and serial connections. The Ethernet connections are simple to set up, but there are still a few items to pay attention to. In the past, Cisco made no assumptions as to which Ethernet media the customer would use, so the interface provided on the older products is AUI only. This interface is useful for a 10Base5 network, but most customers use 10Base2 or 10BaseT, both of which require a transceiver to be attached to the AUI interface to convert the signal and make the physical connection to the network cable.

Newer Cisco products provide a dual-media interface for Ethernet, which you can recognize by the RJ-45 receptacle for a 10BaseT cable alongside an AUI interface. Cisco is not giving you two Ethernets for the price of one here; you can use one or the other, but not both simultaneously. The trick with this one is that the default media type for this interface is AUI, which is probably not the one you want! You will need to configure the router interface explicitly to use the RJ-45 connector. The command to use is MEDIA-TYPE 10BASET.

In most production networks, the serial interfaces would connect the router to a CSU/DSU, which would connect to a WAN service provider's network. The router would be a DTE device and would take a clock signal for that line from the provider's network clock. In the lab there's no provider to give us a clock signal, and there's no CSU/DSU. You will need to do two things to accommodate these differences in order to make the serial connections work in the lab: use back-to-back cable pairs, and configure a clock rate in the router.

Serial interfaces on most Cisco routers use a DB-60 high-density connector on the router end. The cables are called transition cables because the nonrouter end determines its

FROM THE CLASSROOM

electrical signaling. These might be EIA/TIA-232, V.35, X.21, or RS-449. In a production network, the cable you would buy to connect to your CSU/DSU would most likely be a male DTE V.35 cable. If we are making a connection between two routers in the lab, however, there won't be a CSU/DSU, so the male cable will need to connect to a female DCE cable of the same signaling type in a back-to-back arrangement.

Now we have a connection made, but the router needs to get clocking for those connections from somewhere, since we don't have a provider's network to take it from. In the lab, you need to configure one end—the DCE end only—of each serial connection with a clock rate, which will dictate the speed at which the connection will transfer data. Use the CLOCK RATE command for this. The maximum clock rate you can specify will depend on the cable you are using. The V.35 cable will allow a clock rate up to 4 Mbps, while the EIA/TIA-232 will allow only 128 Kbps. You don't need to configure a clock rate on the DTE end of the connection.

A last word about serial cables: Cisco cables list for $100 apiece, so if you are using serial connections in your lab, you will need a $200 cable pair for each one. You might think that you're getting a rugged product for that price, but you're not. There are two pitfalls here: folded pins and upside-down cable attachments. The DB-60 high-density connectors are extremely delicate and the pins will fold up inside very easily if you're careless, ruining the cable. Be sure to watch the orientation of your cables with respect to the router interface before you attach them! The 60 pins are arranged in a matrix with four identical rows of 15 pins each, and the metal sleeve of the D-connector is thin and pliable, so you can physically attach the cable to the router upside down without noticing it. It won't work this way, of course, so you may be in for hours of futile troubleshooting before you discover the problem.

—*By Pamela Forsyth, CCIE, CCSI, CNX*

Wide Area Network Services

WAN services are networks in their own right, just without workstations connected to the link between the two networks. Figure 1-10 shows a WAN link. The purpose of a WAN connection is to be able to transmit

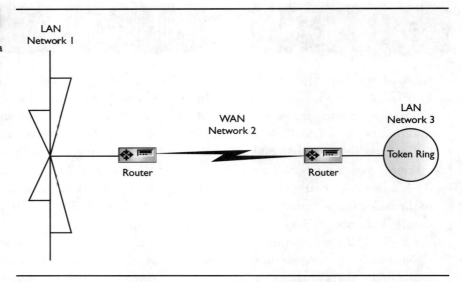

FIGURE 1-10

Two LANs connected by a
WAN link

data between two distant networks as efficiently as possible. The more
efficient the link, the more transparent the connection to the end users.
WAN links are typically slower than LAN links. For example, a T-1 is
1.544 Mbps, while Ethernet 10BaseT is 10 Mbps.

Point to Point

SLIP (Serial Line Internet Protocol) is a legacy UNIX physical layer
protocol for providing serial connections between two networks, or between
a network and a remote node. Because of the universal nature of serial
connection devices and interfaces, such as the RS-232 interface, SLIP was
embraced.

PPP (Point-to-Point Protocol) was designed to address the shortcomings
of SLIP and the need for standard Internet encapsulation protocol. PPP is
the next generation of SLIP, but works at both the physical and the data
link layers. PPP includes enhancements such as encryption, error control,
security, dynamic IP addressing, multiple protocol support, and automatic
connection negotiation. PPP will work over serial lines, ISDN, and
high-speed WAN links. The PPP data frame is shown in Figure 1-11.

FIGURE 1-11

PPP data frame

Flag 01111110	Address 11111111	Control 00000011	Protocol 2 bytes that identify the protocol	Data max 1500 bytes	Frame check sequence 2-or 4-byte field for error handling

In addition to a frame with data, there are other frames that PPP uses. An LCP (Link Control Protocol) frame is used to establish and configure the connection. An NCP (Network Control Protocol) frame is used to select and configure the network layer protocols. Explicit LCP frames are used to close the link.

Frame Relay

Frame Relay is a widely used packet-switched WAN protocol standardized by the ITU-T. Frame Relay relies on the physical and data link layer interface between DTE and DCE devices. Frame Relay networks are either public, and provided by carriers, or privately owned. The key benefit of Frame Relay is the capability to connect with multiple WAN sites through a single link. This makes Frame Relay much cheaper than point-to-point circuits for large WANs. Dedicated point-to-point circuits connect the customer into a nearby Frame Relay switch at the carrier. From there, the Frame Relay switches work like routers, forwarding packets through the carrier's network, based on addressing in the packet header.

Frame Relay is very similar to the X.25 protocol. It uses a virtual circuit—permanent (PVC) or switched (SVC)—between the source and destination, and uses statistical multiplexing for managing multiple data streams. Because of the reliability of the media, error correction is handled at higher protocol layers. There is a CRC to detect and discard corrupted data, but Frame Relay does not request retransmission. Instead Frame Relay relies on higher-level protocols for error correction.

SVCs are temporary links best used in networks with sporadic data transmission. An SVC session begins with a call setup that creates the virtual circuit. Then comes the data transfer, then an idle phase for a defined period, keeping the circuit open in case of more data. Finally, there is a call termination.

PVCs are permanently established links and are the most common implementation of Frame Relay. There are only two session operations, data transfer and idle. The carrier service configures the PVC, since it is routed through the carrier's internetwork. (See Figure 1-12.)

An important concept to know about Frame Relay is *Data Link Connection Identifier* (DLCI). The DLCI is a number used locally by a DTE and assigned by the Frame Relay provider. It refers to the connection between two DTEs in the Frame Relay network. Because it is a local identifier, each DTE may use a different number to identify the link.

In order to maximize throughput, flow control uses a congestion notification method. FECN (forward-explicit congestion notification) is a bit in the frame that is set to 1 when the frame experiences congestion between source and destination. The DTE device sends this information to upper protocol layers in order to begin controlling the flow. BECN (backward-explicit congestion notification) is a bit that is set to 1 when an FECN frame has been received that experienced congestion between source and destination. FECN and BECN are one-bit fields that may be set to 0 as

---

FIGURE 1-12

Carrier's Frame Relay network

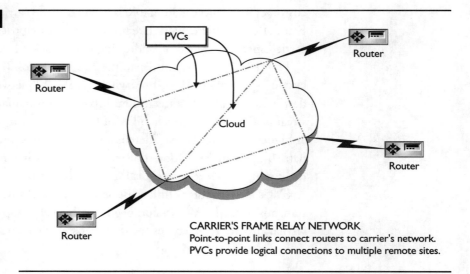

CARRIER'S FRAME RELAY NETWORK
Point-to-point links connect routers to carrier's network.
PVCs provide logical connections to multiple remote sites.

QUESTIONS AND ANSWERS

Shari is configuring the DLCI for a PVC between Portland and Phoenix. The provider gave her two numbers—12 and—14, and assigned them to the link. Shari arbitrarily uses 12 for Portland and 14 for Phoenix. When the link is completely configured, it does not work. Why?	The provider should have specified that the DLCI for Portland was 14 and that the DLCI for Phoenix was 12. The local identifier was wrong and the link did not come up.

well, which means there is no congestion or that the congestion notification feature is not implemented by the switches in the network. The bits exist in the header at all times, no matter what their value. (See Figure 1-13.)

X.25

The ITU-T X.25 standard describes the physical, data link, and network layer protocols for a legacy packet-switching protocol. The physical layer protocol is X.21, which is roughly equivalent to the RS-232 serial interface. The data link layer protocol is LAPB (Link Access Protocol Balanced). The network layer specifies PLP (Packet Level Protocol).

Like Frame Relay, X.25 uses PVCs and SVCs, but its link speeds of 9.6 to 256 Kbps are slower. The data transfer rate is relatively slow compared to newer protocols, because X.25 was defined when media transmission quality was poor. As a result, the protocol specifies that each switching node must fully receive each packet and verify that there are no errors before sending it on to the next node. X.25 may utilize variable-sized packets. As a result of the hop-by-hop error checking and retransmission, and the variable packet size, X.25 is very slow. With the reliability of today's transmission lines, X.25 has a hard time competing with higher-performance protocols, like Frame Relay,

FIGURE 1-13

Frame Relay frame format

Flags	Address DLCI and address information FECN, BECN, and discard eligibility bits	Data

that do not offer guaranteed delivery. Frame Relay has no error recovery at all—errored packets are dropped without notification. Error checking is only done when the Frame Relay frame gets to its final destination.

X.25 uses a point-to-point connection between DTE and DCE. Via a PAD (packet assembler/disassembler), the DTE connects to a carrier-provided DCE, which in turn connects to a packet-switching exchange (PSE or switch), and eventually reaches a destination DTE.

ISDN

Integrated Services Digital Network was standardized by the ITU-T. It was developed as a project to upgrade the Public Switched Telephone Network (PSTN) to a digital service. The physical specification for transmission medium is copper wire.

There are several components to ISDN, as illustrated in Figure 1-14. There is terminal equipment, network termination, and adapters of the following types.

- **TE1 – Terminal Equipment type 1**   ISDN terminals
- **TE2 – Terminal Equipment type 2**   Pre-ISDN type terminals
- **NT1 – Network Termination type 1**   Equipment that connects the subscription 4 wires to the 2 wire local loop
- **NT2 – Network Termination type 2**   Equipment that performs protocol functions of the data link and network layers
- **TA – Terminal Adapter**   Used with a pre-ISDN terminal (TE2) to adapt it to an ISDN connection

When ordering ISDN, consumers usually have the choice between BR (Basic Rate) and PR (Primary Rate) and Hybrid. There are various digital channels that make up these two configurations. The available digital channels are

- **A**   Analog telephone, 4 KHz
- **B**   Digital data, 64 Kbps
- **C**   Digital out-of-band, 8 or 16 Kbps

ISDN equipment connections

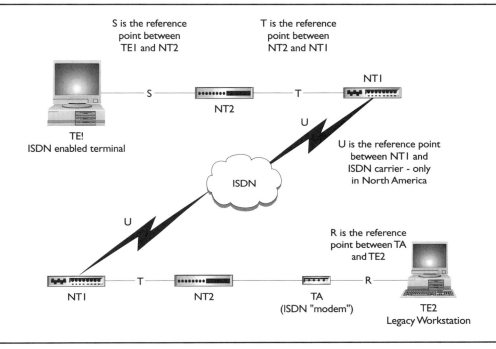

- **D** Digital out-of-band, 16 or 64 Kbps with three subchannels: s (signaling), t (telemetry), and p (packet data)
- **E** Digital channel for internal ISDN signaling, 64 Kbps
- **H** Digital channel at 384 Kbps, 1536 Kbps, or 1920 Kbps

BR consists of two B channels and one D channel, and with control information has an effective bit rate of 192 Kbps. PR consists of one D channel and 23 B channels, with a bandwidth of 1.544 Mbps. In Europe, PR has one D channel and 30 B channels. Hybrid is a single A channel and a single C channel.

Note that LAPD (link access procedure for the D channel) is the signalling protocol used to set up ISDN calls for ISDN BRI at the data link layer.

ATM

ATM (Asynchronous Transfer Mode) is a cell-switching protocol that uses a fixed 53-byte cell length and a cell relay method that reduces transmission delays. ATM can transmit voice, video, and data over variable-speed LAN and WAN links from DS-1 (1.544 Mbps) to as high as 622 Mbps. The key to ATM's high speed is within the fixed cell length. The fixed cell length enables routers to relay cells at the hardware level, using less processing power and increasing the data transmission.

The ITU-T developed ATM as the result of a broadband integrated services signal network study. It evolved further from the work of the ATM Forum founded by Cisco, Net/Adaptive, Northern Telecom, and Sprint. The technology used is VLSI (very large-scale integration), which segments data frames at high speeds into small, fixed units known as cells.

VLSI technology made possible the development of ASICs (application-specific integrated circuits) specifically to perform the segmentation and reassembly of data in hardware rather than in software. Along with the fixed cell size, this is what makes it possible to operate ATM circuits efficiently at such breathtaking speeds, now up to OC-48 (2 Gbps).

The cells relay through ATM switch devices that analyze the cell header and switch it to the correct output interface, in a switch-to-switch path until the cell reaches its final destination. The asynchronous method uses time slots that are available upon demand, rather than strict and wasteful time division multiplexing.

There are two header formats: UNI and NNI (Network Node Interface). UNI is the communication between end nodes and ATM switches. NNI is the communication between two ATM switches. The diagram shown in Figure 1-15 displays the two different header formats.

ATM uses its own reference model, parts of which are analogous to the OSI reference model. The ATM layer and the ATM adaptation layer are roughly equivalent to the data link layer, and the ATM physical layer is analogous to the OSI physical layer.

The ATM physical layer is responsible for the bitstream transmission. The ATM physical layer contains two sublayers: physical medium and transmission convergence. The physical medium transmits the bitstream and timing synchronization information. The physical media that are

UNI and NNI cell
header formats

GFC - Generic flow control	VPI- Virtual path identifier	VCI- Virtual channel identifier	PT- Payload type	CLP- Congestion loss priority	HEC- Header error control

5-byte length UNI cell header

VPI- Virtual path identifier	VCI- Virtual channel identifier	PT- Payload type	CLP- Congestion loss priority	HEC- Header error control

5-byte length NNI cell header

Does not have GFC, instead the larger VPI field allows larger paths.

supported are SONET/SDH, DS-1, DS-3/E3, OC-3, OC-12, 155 Mbps UTP, 100 Mbps FDDI, and 155 Mbps Fiber Channel. The transmission convergence manages cell delineation and header error control data, and packages ATM cells into frames that work with the physical media.

The ATM layer establishes connections and relays cells using the cell header information. It is responsible for mapping network layer addresses to ATM addresses. The ATM adaptation layer (AAL) translates the larger data packets into cells.

ATM is similar to Frame Relay in its switching mechanisms. Instead of switching variable-length packets over PVCs and SVCs, ATM switches fixed-length cells through the internetwork. ATM devices connect directly to an ATM switch.

In order to deliver voice, video, and data in an appropriate fashion, ATM has implemented new features. One of these is called Quality of Service (QoS). Quality of Service allows an ATM device to prioritize data based on the content. Thus, delivery of a file transfer can take a back seat to a video transmission, since the bursty data transfer of the file will not affect the quality of the service. On the other hand, a video transmission that stopped in the middle of a screen would be considered problematic.

CERTIFICATION OBJECTIVE 1.03

Network Layer and Path Determination

The main services provided at the network layer are logical addressing of the node and network segments. As a result, the routing of data between the logical addresses is handled at the network layer. IP of the IP protocol suite is considered a network layer protocol. Data is broken into "packets" at this layer.

The network layer is where internetworking takes place. While the data link layer protocols have features that enable data to be passed from one node to another node on the same link, network layer protocols enable data to be passed from one network to another. This means that the network layer protocols must always contain addressing information that uniquely identifies networks within the internetwork.

Layer 3 Addresses

Networking itself is the capability to share data between two nodes. Being able to simply locate the nodes on the network is one of the most basic and important functions in networking. The network layer not only provides a unique node address, but also a unique network address. This enables the routing of data between networks.

Layer 3, or the network layer, is where addressing is most important. When applying the OSI reference model to the IP protocol suite, IP (Internet Protocol) would be at layer 3. The IP addressing scheme determines the network that a node is on and the logical node address on the network. The logical node address is often *the same* as the MAC address in other protocols, although it is not in IP. This is dealt with on the lower data link layer (layer 2). Note that in Novell IPX, for instance, the MAC address is used for the network layer node address without modification.

A network layer address is also called a *logical address* or *software address*. Network layer addresses are hierarchical, and provide both the network and the node address. A router can easily separate the addresses to be sent on a particular interface by simply looking at the initial network portion of the address—the network address. When the packet reaches the destination network, the node address portion is used to locate the specific station.

Routed Protocols Versus Routing Protocols

Routed protocols are used by end nodes to encapsulate data into packets along with network-layer addressing information so it can be relayed through the internetwork. AppleTalk, IP, and IPX are all routed protocols. When a protocol does not support a network layer address, then it is a nonrouted protocol.

Routers use routing protocols to build and maintain routing tables and to forward data packets along the best path toward their destination networks. Routing protocols enable routers to learn about the status of networks that are not directly connected to them, and to communicate to other routers about the networks they are aware of. This communication is carried out on a continuing basis so the information in the routing table is updated as changes occur in the internetwork.

The characteristics that distinguish one routing protocol from another include

- The routed protocol for which it maintains information

- The way the routers communicate among each other

- How often this communication takes place

- The algorithm and metrics used to determine the best path

- How long it takes for news of a change to be communicated throughout the network

Examples of routing protocols include RTMP, OSPF, and RIP.

Routing Algorithms and Metrics

A routing algorithm is the calculation that the routing protocol uses to determine the best route to a destination network. The simpler the routing algorithm, the less processing power the router will use. This, in turn, keeps the overhead low on the router.

Metrics are values used to determine which route is preferable. Depending on the routing protocol, different factors determine a route's metric, including the number of hops, link speeds, delay, reliability, and load. The resulting metrics are stored with the routes in a routing table or a link-state database.

CERTIFICATION OBJECTIVE 1.04

Transport Layer

The transport layer provides data transport services, effectively shielding the upper layers from data transfer issues. Transport layer services are concerned with the reliability of the connection, establishing virtual circuits, error detection and recovery, and flow control. When the OSI model is applied to the IP protocol suite, TCP and UDP are both transport layer protocols.

Reliability

Transmission Control Protocol (TCP) is considered a *reliable, connection-oriented* protocol. User Datagram Protocol (UDP) is *unreliable* and *connectionless*. The difference between a reliable and unreliable protocol is the acknowledgment to the sender that data has been received. There is more overhead involved with a reliable protocol because of the acknowledgments. On the other hand, unreliable protocols do not guarantee delivery of data, and can be prone to more errors in delivery.

Connectionless, or unreliable, protocols are used quite often when reliability issues such as sequencing and error recovery are addressed at the application layer. The advantage is that because they have fewer features, the overhead is very low.

Windowing

When some transport protocols negotiate a reliable connection between two nodes on an internetwork, they also negotiate a moving target of the amount of data that can be transmitted at any one time. That moving target is called a *sliding window*. This process is called *Windowing*.

CERTIFICATION OBJECTIVE 1.05

Upper-Layer Protocols

The term *upper-layer protocols* refers to the session, presentation, and application layer protocols. The application layer provides basic services such as file transfer and network management to applications. It establishes the availability of destination nodes, and identifies the application synchronization between the nodes.

Presentation layer is aptly named, for this layer handles the formatting of data, or presentation of that data. Services in the presentation layer include data encryption. The presentation layer protocol can also negotiate the syntax of the data in order for translation to occur with the destination node.

As the name implies, the session layer establishes the session between two network nodes, maintains it, and terminates it as well. Services at this layer include class of service, data prioritization, and reporting errors for the upper two layers.

CERTIFICATION OBJECTIVE 1.06

Cisco Routers, Switches, and Hubs

Cisco IOS Software (Internetworking Operating System) is the software that runs on the Cisco products. This platform is integral to the interoperations of network devices in a Cisco internetwork. Cisco IOS includes security, access control, authentication, firewall, encryption, management services, and support for IBM connectivity, switching, voice and multimedia, and quality of service. The main purpose of IOS is to boot the Cisco hardware and begin the optimal transport of data across the internetwork.

Of the internetwork routers available from Cisco, the Gigabit Switched 12000 series routers are built to handle the fastest backbone traffic. Gigabit switched traffic is standard, where the backbones of these routers can handle up to 4, 8 or 12 cards (depending on which router selected) that are OC-3 to OC-48 compliant. The target networks for a Gigabit Switched 12000 series router running Cisco IOS are Internet service providers, enterprise WAN backbones, and other high-throughput internetworks needing speeds of even 2.4 Gbps and up. It supports SONET, ATM, and DS-3/E-3 connections.

The platform for multiprotocol routers is the Cisco 7000 series routers, which run the Cisco IOS. The 7500 high-end series features Cisco Extended Bus (Cybus), which is connected to the external network through network interfaces connected to modular interface processors. The 7500 series supports any combination of the following.

- ATM
- Channelized T3
- FDDI
- Multichannel T1/E1
- HSSI
- Packet OC-3
- Synchronous serial
- Token Ring
- Ethernet
- Fast Ethernet

In order to avoid network service interruption, the 7500 series supports online software reconfiguration without rebooting, online insertion and removal of new interface processors without rebooting, a fast boot process, self-diagnostics, and dual power supply options for some of the versions.

Cisco offers several routers built to provide the price and performance needed in smaller, workgroup-oriented LANs and WANs. These routers include the 2500 series, the 3600 series, and the 4000 series. They support the most widely used protocols and physical media, from Ethernet and Token Ring to FDDI.

Switching services are becoming more popular due to the immediate speed improvements they can bring to a LAN. Switches can be connected to hubs or directly to workstations and servers. The algorithms used to determine the location of a hardware device effectively give each port a full throughput of 10 Mbps on Ethernet 10BaseT LANs.

Catalyst 1900/2820 switch is a flexible switch that can be integrated in anything from a small LAN to an enterprise WAN. It includes three switching modes: fastforward, fragmentfree, and store and forward. The fastforward mode begins forwarding a frame as soon as the MAC address is learned. Fragmentfree mode begins forwarding a frame as soon as it reaches 64 bytes, which is determined to be the threshold for fragment size. And store and forward receives the complete frame and checks it for errors before forwarding it. Fastforward is the default, as well as fastest mode. Store and forward is automatically used for packets travelling between 10 Mbps ports and 100 Mbps ports. The mode must be set for the switch if fastforward is not desired. The spanning tree protocol (IEEE 802.1d standard) is used for transparently reconfiguring the switch when the network topology changes.

Hubs are also available from Cisco in the FastHub Series. FastHubs are Ethernet hubs that can be used alone, stacked together in a LAN workgroup, or connected to Catalyst Switches to form VLANs (Virtual Local Area Network). Other Cisco products available include: Frame Relay PAD/routers, access routers for remote access users, ISDN routers, ATM switches, firewalls, and other network management hardware solutions.

Configuring a Cisco Switch and Hub

For any type of switch or hub, the following instructions apply:

- Unpack the hardware and verify the contents matches the packing list.

- Stack or rack-mount (with the correct rubber feet or rack hardware) the switch in a location that is no more than 100 meters from any attached 10BaseT device, where the temperature is correct for the product, with sufficient airflow.

- When selecting cables, use straight-through cables for all ports *not* marked with an X. The X stands for crossover cables. Category 5 cables will work for all ports except for the 100BaseFX port, which requires fiber-optic media.

- Verify that the voltage of the power outlet is the same as the voltage indicated on the label, and connect the power.

There is a method to setting up a Cisco Catalyst 2820 switch. This method demonstrates out-of-band management. That is, it manages the switch from a terminal that is directly connected to a serial port on the switch. This method has the advantage of working regardless of whether network connectivity is available from the switch. The steps to setting up a Cisco Catalyst 2820 switch are

1. Turn on the switch and watch POST (power on self-test), in which all the port LEDs should turn Green and then Off.

2. Connect the devices to the hub using the correct cables.

3. Connect a VT-100 terminal or emulator to the EIA/TIA-232 (RS-232) port, using the settings for 9600 bps, 8 data bits, 1 stop bit, and no parity, and log in.

4. Press S to access the System Configuration menu, and change the Switching Mode by selecting S again. Then select the number for the

switching mode desired. This step is unnecessary if fastforward switching is desired.

5. Press X to exit to the main menu and then press N to access the Network Management menu, which is where the protocol configuration is.

6. Press I to access IP Configuration, then press I again to assign an IP address. When assigning an IP address any time after the first assignment, the switch must be reset for the address to take effect. Select S and G to assign the appropriate subnet mask and Default Gateway, respectively.

7. Press X to exit to the Main menu, select S again for the System, and press R to reset the switch and retain the assigned parameters.

Installing a FastHub 316C or FastHub 316T begins with the same unpacking and verification procedures as the switch installation. After unpacking and physically installing the hub, it can be further configured.

1. After plugging in the hub, and verifying POST, connect the devices to the RJ-45 ports.

2. Connect a node to the console port, and configure the terminal emulation program for 9600 baud, 8 data bits, 1 stop bit, and no parity.

3. At the management console, log in.

4. Select the IP Configuration menu. Set the IP address, subnet mask, default gateway, and DNS server. Disable RIP if another routing protocol is being used.

5. Exit to the Main menu and Exit the console.

CERTIFICATION SUMMARY

A model for internetworks had to answer the challenges of interoperability and interconnectivity. These challenges prompted the development of a layered protocol model, both as a standardized model and one that was accepted due to its popular use. TCP/IP developed as a four-layer popular model. The seven-layer OSI reference model was developed and standardized by the ISO. The seven layers of the OSI model are application, presentation, session, transport, network, data link, and physical. Data travels through the protocol layers at the source by being broken into smaller data units and having header information added for each layer. When the data is reassembled and passed to the upper protocols at the destination, the header is discarded for each layer that the data has passed through. This allows independence of layers from each other. The header addition for each protocol layer is called encapsulation.

The physical layer is responsible for the bitstream of data, and its transmission. The data link layer consists of two sublayers: Logical Link Control and Media Access Control. The MAC sublayer handles hardware addressing—MAC addresses. The LLC sublayer handles control information in the frames, which are the data units at the data link layer.

The IEEE (Institute for Electrical and Electronics Engineers) created an 802 series of standards for physical and data link layer protocols. These included the standards for Ethernet (802.3) and for Token Ring (802.5), among others. ANSI (American National Standards Institute) created FDDI, a physical and data link layer standard that uses optical fiber media.

Ethernet, originally created by DIX (Digital/Intel/Xerox) is a CSMA/CD protocol allowing all nodes access to the network. If a collision occurs, the protocol has a method of sensing the collision and retransmitting the data. Ethernet can use thick or thin coax or unshielded twisted-pair copper wire. The rate of data transmission is usually 10 Mbps, however, 1Base5 is 1 Mbps. The most common form of Ethernet is 10BaseT, but 100BaseT is gaining in popularity.

Token Ring is a token-passing ring topology that is wired in a star fashion. IBM initially developed Token Ring. The physical medium used is generally shielded or unshielded twisted-pair copper wire. In this protocol, any station that has data to send must wait until a token frame is received. When the token is received, that station may send the data. The receiving station copies the data and changes a bit on the header, then forwards that data on to the original sending node. When the sending node receives the frame, it releases the token and checks the header to see if the data was received at its destination. With Token Ring, there are no collisions, so data is only retransmitted if a frame is damaged.

FDDI (Fiber Distributed Data Interface) is a dual ring token-passing protocol, similar to Token Ring, based on fiber-optic media. This has high-capacity speed for 100 Mbps. The dual ring topology uses a similar token-passing mechanism to Token Ring, but includes the capacity for fault management by creating a single ring. FDDI can be installed without using hubs, and it uses the secondary fiber ring to recover from failures in the primary ring.

There are several physical interfaces used for connecting nodes to a network. The most prevalent of interfaces is the RS-232 serial interface. V.35 is a physical layer protocol. HSSI is a high-speed serial interface suitable for WAN connections. BRI interfaces are used to connect to an ISDN line.

WAN links include Point-to-Point Protocol, which is a standard IP protocol used to encapsulate data over IP, and can be used over serial connections. Frame Relay is a packet network standard. X.25 is a legacy packet network standard that is very slow as a result of its error checking at each packet switch in the data path. ISDN connects to the digital telephone network. ATM is a cell-switching protocol for high-speed LAN and WANs.

The network layer defines logical addresses for network nodes. Routed protocols support network and node addressing at this layer, enabling packets to be routed through the network. Routing protocols determine the path between two networks by using routing algorithms and metrics, and by advertising their routes.

The transport layer handles reliability of data transfer, and can negotiate a sliding window of data transmission in order to maximize throughput on a network.

The upper-layer protocols—application, presentation, and session—handle the data from the application, its format (such as encryption), and the session settings between the source and destination nodes.

✓ TWO-MINUTE DRILL

- ❑ A potential CCNA must have the knowledge to install, configure, and operate simple-routed LAN, routed WAN, and switched LAN and LANE networks.

- ❑ Internetworking is the process and methodology applied to connecting multiple networks, regardless of their physical topologies and distance.

- ❑ Interconnectivity is the means of transporting information between the computers, inclusive of the physical media, the data packaging mechanism, and the routing between multiple network equipment pieces from the starting node until reaching the destination node.

- ❑ Interoperability is the methodology applied to make data understandable to computers that use proprietary or simply different computer operating systems and languages.

- ❑ The OSI reference model provides a hierarchical tool for understanding networking technology, as well as a basis for current and future network developments.

- ❑ The OSI model is a seven-layer protocol suite model.

- ❑ A common mnemonic device for remembering the layers (application, presentation, session, transport, network, data link, physical) in the right order is **A**ll **P**eople **S**eem **T**o **N**eed **D**ata **P**rocessing.

- ❑ Encapsulation is the process of adding a header to the data, or *wrapping* the data.

- ❑ The physical layer, or layer 1, defines the actual mechanical specifications and electrical data bitstream.

- ❑ The data link layer, or layer 2, is also known as the link layer. It consists of two sublayers, the upper level being the Logical Link Control (LLC), and the lower level being the Media Access Control (MAC).

- ❑ 802.3 specifies the physical layer and the MAC portion of the data link layer, while DIX Ethernet specifies the entire physical and

❑ data link layers. 802.3 specifies different physical layers, but DIX Ethernet only specifies one.

❑ Token Ring networks are nearly identical and compatible with the IEEE 802.5 specification developed later, which was based on IBM's Token Ring.

❑ The FDDI standard specifies the physical and MAC portion of the data link layers for a token-passing, dual-ring topology using fiber-optic media at 100 Mbps.

❑ Interfaces are used to connect data terminal equipment (DTE) and data circuit-terminating equipment (DCE) devices.

❑ In the RS-232 serial port, one pin is used to transmit data, another to receive data.

❑ The V.35 standard is a physical layer protocol suitable for connections to a packet network at speeds up to 48 Kbps, and beyond, even to 4 Mbps.

❑ HSSI is a DTE/DCE interface that handles high-speed communication over WAN links.

❑ BRI (Basic Rate Interface) is an ISDN (Integrated Services Digital Network) term for an ISDN connection consisting of two B channels at 64 Kbps and one D channel at 16 Kbps.

❑ Synchronizing network timing is handled at the physical layer of the OSI reference model.

❑ The purpose of a WAN connection is to be able to transmit data between two distant networks as efficiently as possible.

❑ SLIP (Serial Line Internet Protocol) is a legacy UNIX physical layer protocol for providing serial connections between two networks, or between a network and a remote node.

❑ PPP includes enhancements such as encryption, error control, security, dynamic IP addressing, multiple protocol support, and automatic connection negotiation. PPP will work over serial lines, ISDN, and high-speed WAN links.

❑ Frame Relay is a widely used packet-switched WAN protocol standardized by the ITU-T. Frame Relay relies on the physical and data link layer interface between DTE and DCE devices.

❑ The ITU-T X.25 standard describes the physical, data link, and network layer protocols for a legacy packet-switching protocol.

❑ Integrated Services Digital Network was developed as a project to upgrade the Public Switched Telephone Network (PSTN) to a digital service.

❑ ATM (Asynchronous Transfer Mode) is a cell-switching protocol that uses a fixed 53-byte cell length and a cell relay method that reduces transmission delays.

❑ The main services provided at the network layer are logical addressing of the node and network segments.

❑ Layer 3, or the network layer, is where addressing is most important.

❑ Routed protocols are used by end nodes to encapsulate data into packets along with network-layer addressing information so it can be relayed through the internetwork.

❑ A routing algorithm is the calculation that the routing protocol uses to determine the best route to a destination network.

❑ The transport layer provides data transport services, effectively shielding the upper layers from data transfer issues.

❑ Transmission Control Protocol (TCP) is considered a *reliable*, *connection-oriented* protocol. User Datagram Protocol (UDP) is *unreliable* and *connectionless*.

❑ The term upper-layer protocols refers to the session, presentation, and application layer protocols.

❑ Cisco IOS Software (Internetworking Operating System) is the software that runs on the Cisco products. This platform is integral to the interoperations of network devices in a Cisco internetwork.

SELF TEST

The Self-Test questions will help you measure your understanding of the material presented in this chapter. Read all the choices carefully, as there may be more than one correct answer. Choose all correct answers for each question.

1. What were the two challenges of creating a network model? (Select two.)

    A. Interconnectivity

    B. Interaction

    C. Internetworking

    D. Interoperability

2. The Advanced Research Projects Agency created what network?

    A. Ethernet

    B. FDDI

    C. ARPANET

    D. Token Ring

3. What does OSI stand for?

    A. Organization for Standards Institute

    B. Organization for Internet Standards

    C. Open Standards Institute

    D. Open Systems Interconnection

4. What are the layers of the OSI reference model, in order?

    A. Application, transport, network, physical

    B. Application, presentation, session, network, transport, data link, physical

    C. Application, presentation, session, transport, network, data link, physical

    D. Application, session, transport, physical

5. What is the term for wrapping a data unit with a header and passing it to the next protocol?

    A. Windowing

    B. Encapsulation

    C. Wrapping

    D. Heading

6. Which of the following is not defined at the physical layer of the OSI reference model?

    A. Hardware addresses

    B. Bitstream transmission

    C. Voltage levels

    D. Physical interface

7. Which standards institute created the 802 series of physical/data link layer standards?

    A. ANSI

    B. DIX

    C. ITU-T

    D. IEEE

8. Who created Ethernet?

    A. ANSI

    B. DIX

    C. ITU-T

    D. IEEE

9. What is the function of CSMA/CD?

    A. It passes a token around a star topology.

B. Nodes access the network and retransmit if they detect a collision.

C. Nodes connect to a dual ring of fiber-optics and use a token-passing scheme.

D. Nodes break the frames into tiny cells and forward them through a cell-switching network.

10. What is a backoff algorithm?

A. It is the fault tolerance calculation for FDDI.

B. It is a routing calculation for determining the best route.

C. It is the notification that a serious error has occurred on the network.

D. It is the duration calculation to delay retransmission after a collision, before retransmitting in Ethernet.

11. IBM's Token Ring specification is nearly identical and compatible with IEEE's 802.5 specification.

A. True

B. False

12. What is beaconing?

A. It is the fault tolerance calculation for FDDI.

B. It is a routing calculation for determining the best route.

C. It is the notification that a serious error has occurred on the network.

D. It is the duration calculation to delay retransmission after a collision, before retransmitting in Ethernet.

13. What two types of frames are found on a Token Ring network?

A. Token

B. Frame check sequence

C. Data

D. Address

14. The FDDI specification includes which layers of the OSI reference model?

A. Physical and network

B. Physical and transport

C. Physical and MAC sublayer of data link

D. Physical and data link

15. What is RS-232?

A. A standard serial port interface

B. A high-speed serial interface

C. An ISDN interface

D. An ATM switch

16. What is the maximum data transmission rate for HSSI?

A. 64 Kbps

B. 256 Kbps

C. 100 Mbps

D. 52 Mbps

17. What does the hierarchical network-layer address provide?

A. The hardware address

B. The node address and the hardware address

C. The network address and the node address

D. The network address mapped to the hardware address

18. What qualities match TCP?

    A. Connectionless, reliable
    B. Connection-oriented, reliable
    C. Connectionless, unreliable
    D. Connection-oriented, unreliable

19. What layer of the OSI reference model specifies data formats, such as encryption?

    A. Application
    B. Presentation
    C. Session
    D. Transport
    E. Network
    F. Data link
    G. Physical

20. What is out-of-band management?

    A. It is the ability to manage a switch or hub from a networked workstation.
    B. It is the addition of a network management module to a hub.
    C. It is the fault tolerance feature of the dual ring FDDI creating a single ring.
    D. It is the ability to manage a device using a connection other than the network.

21. Interoperability means

    A. Transfer of data between systems
    B. Ability to make data understandable by machines that use different operating systems, hardware, or languages
    C. Agreement between two equipment vendors for processing data
    D. Ability of LAN to communicate with WAN

22. OSI is what kind of standard?

    A. A standard created by major telecommunications service providers
    B. A de facto standard
    C. A de jure standard
    D. A standard created by major equipment manufacturers

23. The layered approach of the OSI results in

    A. Increased development costs for a specific vendor product
    B. Increased marketability for a specific vendor product
    C. A hierarchical tool for network architecture
    D. All of the above
    E. B and C only
    F. A and C only

24. Which of the following statements is true in general when an application at the source wishes to send data to an application at the destination address?

    A. The lower layer at destination adds its own header information to the data it receives from the higher layer.

B. The lower layer at source adds its own header information to the data it receives from the higher layer.

C. The lower layer at destination strips header information from the data added by the higher layer.

D. The higher layer at source strips header information added to the data by the lower layer.

25. In the OSI model, encapsulation of the data may occur at

   A. Layer 7 of the source

   B. Layer 1 of the destination

   C. Layer 7 of the destination

   D. All layers at source

   E. Layer 1 of the source

26. The session layer functionality in the OSI model is usually implemented

   A. At user premises

   B. In hardware

   C. In software

   D. In hardware and software

27. At the physical layer in the OSI model the data is broken into

   A. Cells

   B. Fragments

   C. Bits

   D. Packets

28. Collision in a CSMA/CD network is said to occur when

   A. A node listens to the network and hears nothing.

B. A node receives a message from the network.

C. Two nodes hear nothing and then transmit data simultaneously.

D. A node on the network has physical failure.

29. A broadcast system means

   A. Only few nodes on the network see the data meant for these nodes.

   B. All nodes on the network see all the data frames.

   C. Network informs all the nodes of a network failure.

   D. None of the above.

30. Which statements are true of a preamble in the IEEE 802.3 frame?

   A. It is an indication that a node is receiving a new frame.

   B. It contains all 0's

   C. It contains all 1's

   D. It contains alternating 0's and 1's

   E. A and B only

   F. A and D only

   G. A and C only

31. A Frame Check Sequence (FCS) in the IEEE 802.3 frame includes

   A. A receiving station address

   B. A source station address

   C. A Cyclic Redundancy Check (CRC) value

   D. A sequence number of the frame

32. In a Token Ring network architecture, what does it mean when a node possesses a token?

    A. The node has the ability to transmit the data to the network.

    B. The node has the right to pass the data to the network.

    C. The node has the right to retain the token.

    D. None of the above.

33. In a Token Ring network architecture, if a node receives a token and has data to transmit, then

    A. The node does nothing.

    B. The node waits for data to be transmitted.

    C. The node converts the token into a start-of-frame field.

    D. None of the above.

34. What is the main purpose of the dual ring architecture in Fiber Distributed Data Interface (FDDI)?

    A. To increase traffic on the network

    B. To allow bidirectional traffic on the network

    C. To provide fault tolerance

    D. To provide one path for traffic from selected nodes

35. Which statement is true of the Media Access Control (MAC) address?

    A. It is dependent on the hardware location.

    B. It is dependent on the network type.

    C. It is assigned by a vendor.

    D. It changes every time the hardware is plugged turned on and off.

36. The Basic Rate Interface (BRI) in ISDN has

    A. One B channel and one D channel

    B. 23 B channels and one D channel

    C. Two B channels and one D channel

    D. Two D channels and one B channel

37. Synchronization of network timing is done at which layer?

    A. Data link layer

    B. Transport layer

    C. Physical layer

    D. Session layer

38. What is a Network Control Protocol (NCP) frame in a Point-to-Point Protocol (PPP) used for?

    A. Establishing and configuring a connection

    B. Encryption of data

    C. Assigning a dynamic address

    D. Selecting and configuring the network layer protocol

39. In a Frame Relay network, which statement is true of Forward Explicit Congestion (FECN) when the network is congested?

    A. It is a bit that is set to 0.

    B. It is a bit that is set to 1.

C. It is sent by DTE to upper protocol layers.

D. A and C only.

E. B and C only.

40. Data Link Connection Identifier (DLCI) in a Frame Relay network identifies what?

A. Data Terminal Equipment (DTE)

B. Data Circuit Termination Equipment (DCE)

C. A connection between two DTEs

D. All of the above

41. How does a Permanent Virtual Circuit (PVC) in a Frame Relay network differ from a Switched Virtual Circuit (SVC)?

A. It is a permanently established link.

B. It terminates after the call has ended.

C. It has a data transfer phase.

D. It has an idle phase.

42. The ITU X.25 Standard describes protocol for which layer or layers?

A. Physical layer

B. Session layer

C. Transport layer

D. Data link layer

E. Network layer

F. A, B and C only

G. A, D and E only

H. A, C and D only

43. X.25 can handle data rates up to

A. 1024 Kbps

B. 256 Kbps

C. 512 Kbps

D. 768 Kbps

44. Asynchronous Transfer Mode (ATM) is a

A. Packet-switching technology

B. Frame-switching technology

C. Cell-switching technology

D. Circuit-switching technology

45. How many header formats are there in ATM terminology?

A. 5

B. 4

C. 3

D. 2

E. 1

46. Which of the following uses Internetwork Operating System (IOS)?

A. Bridges

B. DMS-100

C. 4ESS

D. Cisco routers

E. 5ESS

47. How many switching modes are included in Catalyst 1900/2820 switches?

A. 1

B. 2

C. 3

D. 4

2

Getting Started with Cisco IOS Software

A router needs to be configured in order to operate within your network. Once it is configured, network operators often need to check the status of various router components. In this chapter, you will learn about the configurable components of a router and how to use the features of the user interface to configure the router and to verify your configuration. You will also learn how to do some basic network testing using the Cisco IOS diagnostic capabilities and how to gain remote access to other routers over the network. Finally, you will learn several techniques for manipulating configuration files.

CERTIFICATION OBJECTIVE 2.01

User Interface

The most common way to interact with the router is through the command-line interface provided by the Cisco IOS software. Every Cisco router has a console port that can be directly connected to a PC or terminal so that you can type commands at the keyboard and receive output on a terminal screen. The term *console* refers to this keyboard and screen that are directly attached to the router. The part of the Cisco IOS software that provides the user interface and interprets the commands you type is called the command executive, or EXEC.

This section will teach you how to log in to the router, use the features provided by the user interface, and log out of the router again. It will also introduce the two primary modes of interacting with the router: user EXEC mode and privileged EXEC mode.

User and Privileged Modes

If you walk up to a router console that has been idle for some time, you will see a screen displaying the following lines:

```
east con0 is now available
Press RETURN to get started.
```

In order to begin working with the router from the console you will need to log in. If you press ENTER, you will be prompted for a password.

```
User Access Verification
Password:
Router>
```

You will not see the password characters appear on the console screen.

Once you have successfully entered the console password, you will see the prompt Router>. The router is now waiting for you to type a command at the console keyboard. Router is the default host name for all Cisco routers; the angle bracket following the host name is a signal to you that you are in *user EXEC mode* (user mode). This is the lowest level of access to the router and allows you to examine the status of most of the router's configurable components, see the contents of routing tables, and do basic nondisruptive network troubleshooting. You cannot change the router's configuration in user EXEC mode, nor can you view the contents of the router's configuration files. You should always use this mode for interacting with the router unless you actually need to change your router's configuration, or if you need to do disruptive testing on your network.

The highest level of access to the router is *privileged EXEC mode,* sometimes called enable mode, because the command you use to get into this mode is ENABLE. Here is what you would see at the router console as you enter privileged EXEC mode:

```
Router>enable
Password:
Router#
```

Notice how the prompt changes. You can confirm you are in privileged EXEC mode by the pound sign (#) after the router name. At this level you have full access to the router. In privileged EXEC mode, you have all the commands available for basic troubleshooting and status checking that you had in user EXEC mode, plus commands that enable you to change the router's configuration, perform testing that could potentially disrupt network traffic, reboot the router, and view the configuration files.

To leave privileged EXEC mode and revert to user EXEC mode, use the command DISABLE.

```
Router#disable
Router>
```

Notice how the prompt changes back to the angle bracket. To log out of the router entirely and end your console session, use the command EXIT or LOGOUT. Once you are logged out of the router, the console screen will once again display the idle console message instructing you to press ENTER to get started.

The Command-Line Interface

Let's log back in to our router again and learn how to use the context-sensitive Help feature. This is a feature that you will learn to depend on as you work with the command-line interface.

If you want to know all the commands available to you at any time, just enter a question mark (?) at the prompt. Here is a partial listing of commands available in user EXEC mode:

```
router>?
Exec commands:
  access-enable   Create a temporary Access-List entry
  clear           Reset functions
  connect         Open a terminal connection
  disable         Turn off privileged commands
  disconnect      Disconnect an existing network connection
  enable          Turn on privileged commands
  exit            Exit from the EXEC
  help            Description of the interactive help system
  lat             Open a lat connection
  lock            Lock the terminal
  login           Log in as a particular user
  logout          Exit from the EXEC
  mrinfo          Request neighbor and version information
                  from a multicast router
  mstat           Show statistics after multiple multicast
                  traceroutes
  mtrace          Trace reverse multicast path from
                  destination to source
```

```
  name-connection   Name an existing network connection
  pad               Open a X.29 PAD connection
  ping              Send echo messages
  ppp               Start IETF Point-to-Point Protocol (PPP)
  resume            Resume an active network connection
-More-
```

This display goes on for another screen or two. The "More" at the bottom of the display means that you may see the next screen of output by pressing the SPACEBAR or see one additional line by pressing the ENTER key. Any other keypress will abort the display.

Now let's get into privileged EXEC mode and see how this display differs.

```
Router>enable
Password:
Router#?
Exec commands:
  access-enable     Create a temporary Access-List entry
  access-template   Create a temporary Access-List entry
  bfe               For manual emergency modes setting
  clear             Reset functions
  clock             Manage the system clock
  configure         Enter configuration mode
  connect           Open a terminal connection
  copy              Copy configuration or image data
  debug             Debugging functions (see also 'undebug')
  disable           Turn off privileged commands
  disconnect        Disconnect an existing network connection
  enable            Turn on privileged commands
  erase             Erase flash or configuration memory
  exit              Exit from the EXEC
  help              DEscription of the interactive help system
  lat               Open a lat connection
  lock              Lock the terminal
  login             Log in as a particular user
  logout            Exit from the EXEC
  mbranch           Trace multicast route down tree branch
  mrbranch          Trace reverse multicast route up tree
                    branch
  -More-
```

Many commands you will be using have many parts or *arguments*. The command executive uses a real-time interpreter to execute the commands you type at the console, and it checks the syntax of each one for correctness as you enter it. You can use this syntax checking, along with the context-sensitive Help feature, to learn what information the router expects you to type at any point in any command. Let's look at the example command, CLOCK SET.

```
Router#clk
Translating "clk"...domain server (255.255.255.255) % Name lookup aborted
```

The first thing to notice is that I am in privileged EXEC mode here. You can't set your router's clock from user EXEC mode. I made a mistake in typing the command. If the router sees a word it doesn't recognize as a command, it thinks you are specifying the name of an IP host you want to Telnet to over the network and tries to resolve the host name to an IP address. If you don't have a DNS server on your network, this process takes several seconds to time out. If you want to abort the name lookup, as I did here, use the keystrokes CTRL-SHIFT-6.

Now I want to find out which commands begin with cl. I can do that by typing cl?. There is no space between the l and the question mark.

```
Router#cl?
clear  clock
```

Now I can use the question mark to find out the arguments I need to use for the CLOCK SET command. Watch the space between the last argument on the line and the question mark.

```
Router#clock ?
set  Set the time and date
Router#clock set ?
hh:mm:ss  Current Time
Router#clock set 17:50:00
% Incomplete command.
Router#clock set 17:50:00 ?
 <1-31>  Day of the month
 MONTH   Month of the year
Router#clock set 17:50:00 1
 % Incomplete command.
Router#clock set 17:50:00 1 ?
```

```
MONTH   Month of the year
Router#clock set 17:50:00 1 August
% Incomplete command.
Router#clock set 17:50:00 1 August ?
 <1993-2035>  Year
Router#clock set 17:50:00 1 August 1998
Router#
```

When I get the router prompt back again with no error message, I know the command was correct in syntax.

Some of the commands you will type are very long. It is helpful to know some of the keystrokes that are available to you for moving around on the line you are working on. This feature is known as *enhanced editing.* If you are familiar with UNIX, you will recognize these keystrokes as the emacs editing keystrokes.

- ■ **CTRL-A**   Go to the beginning of the line.
- ■ **CTRL-E**   Go to the end of the line.
- ■ **ESC-B**   Go back, to the beginning of the previous word.
- ■ **ESC-F**   Go forward, to the beginning of the next word.
- ■ **CTRL-B**   Go back one character.
- ■ **CTRL-F**   Go forward one character.

If you are using a VT-100 terminal emulation, you may use the LEFT and RIGHT ARROW keys on your keyboard to move along the line. Use the DELETE and BACKSPACE keys to change characters on the line. Once you press the ENTER key, the command will take effect.

Enhanced editing also includes a feature that scrolls long lines to one side if they are longer than the terminal screen width. This is indicated by a $ next to the prompt, like so:

```
Router>$n extra long line to show how it scrolls under the router prompt
```

As soon as the line you are typing exceeds the width of the terminal screen, characters will appear to scroll under the router prompt. Use the CTRL-A keystroke to get back quickly to the beginning of the line.

If you don't want to use the enhanced editing feature, you may turn it off with the command TERMINAL NO EDITING. To enable it again, use the command TERMINAL EDITING.

The router keeps the last 10 commands you entered during your console or terminal session in a special memory buffer called the *command history*. You may recall commands from the command history and reuse them or change them slightly to save yourself some typing. To see all the commands in the buffer, use the SHOW HISTORY command:

```
Router#show history
conf t
  show interfaces serial
  show interfaces
  show run
  clk
  clock set 17:50:00
  clock set 17:50:00 1
  clock set 17:50:00 1 August
  clock set 17:50:00 1 August 1999
  show history
Router#
```

Notice the commands are recalled exactly as they were typed, even if they were incomplete or erroneous.

You can recall the commands to the command line by moving backward and forward within the history buffer. CTRL-P recalls the previous command in the buffer, and CTRL-N recalls the next command in the buffer. If your terminal is using a VT-100 emulation, you can use the UP and DOWN ARROW keys to move backward and forward within the buffer. Use the TERMINAL HISTORY SIZE command to change the size of the history buffer. For example, to increase the size of the buffer so it will store 100 lines instead of the default, enter the following:

```
Router#terminal history size 100
Router#
```

CERTIFICATION OBJECTIVE 2.02

Router Basics

A router is a computer and has hardware elements that are similar to those of other computers. If you buy a PC from the local computer store, it will have

- A processor (CPU)
- Various sorts of memory, which it uses for storing information
- An operating system, which provides functionality
- Various ports and interfaces to connect it to peripheral devices or to allow it to communicate with other computers

A router has these same elements. In this section, we will learn about the configurable hardware elements of the router, how to configure them, and how to check their status.

Router Elements

Before we power up the router we need to understand some of its components. The hardware components of the router include memory, processor, lines, and interfaces.

The Cisco router uses the following types of memory:

- **Random-access memory (RAM)** Stores the running (or active) configuration file; routing; and other tables and packet buffers. The Cisco IOS software executes from main memory.
- **Flash memory** Stores the operating system software image, or IOS image.

- **Nonvolatile RAM (NVRAM)** Special memory that does not lose its information when the router is powered off. Stores the system's startup configuration file and the virtual configuration register.

- **Read-only memory (ROM)** The image in ROM is the image the router first uses when it is powered up. This image is usually an older and smaller version of IOS without the features of a full IOS version.

The whole point of a router is to forward packets from one network to another, so it stands to reason that a router's interfaces will be of primary interest to us. Interfaces are those elements that physically connect the router to various types of networks. Some of the most common router interfaces are serial (which generally connect the router to wide-area links) and the LAN interfaces: Ethernet, Token Ring, and FDDI.

The final category of router component is the one that allows us to interact with the router. We have already learned about the console port, which connects the router to a local terminal. The router also has an auxiliary port, which is often used to connect the router to a modem for out-of-band management in case the network connections are down and the console is inaccessible.

Router Modes

The router's command executive has a hierarchy of modes that limit and organize the commands available to you, the user, as you configure the router. You have already learned the primary router modes, user EXEC mode and privileged EXEC mode, which can be used to check the router's operating status and troubleshoot your network. In order to configure the router, however, we need to understand the configuration modes and how to move among them.

You cannot change the router's configuration from user EXEC mode; so, if you need to configure the router, you first must enter privileged EXEC mode.

Once you are in privileged EXEC mode, you may enter *global configuration mode.* This is the mode you would use to accomplish such tasks as naming your router, configuring a banner message for users logging in to the router, and enabling various routed protocols. Any configuration command that affects the operation of the entire router would be entered in global configuration mode.

Enter global configuration mode by using the command CONFIGURE TERMINAL.

```
Router#configure terminal
Enter configuration commands, one per line. End with CNTL/Z.
Router(config)#hostname MyRouter
MyRouter(config)#
```

Notice how the prompt changes to remind you that you are in global configuration mode, instead of privileged EXEC mode.

To exit global configuration mode and get back to privileged EXEC mode, use the command EXIT or the keystroke CTRL-Z.

The commands take effect immediately when you press the ENTER key and are placed in the running configuration in RAM, which is controlling operation of the router. You can see in the preceding display that as soon as the HOSTNAME command was entered, the router's prompt changed to reflect the new name.

Most users want to check their running configuration right away to see if the new command is reflected in it properly. If you want to do this, remember that you can't use any SHOW commands in global configuration mode, or in any other configuration mode for that matter. You must first exit back to privileged EXEC mode to use the SHOW commands.

Of course, you will want to configure the specific elements of your router. In order to do this, you must first be in global configuration mode. All other configuration modes are entered from global configuration mode. Some of the more frequently used additional configuration modes available, with their special prompts, include

- **Interface configuration mode**   Router(config-if)#
- **Sub-interface configuration mode**   Router(config-subif)#
- **Line configuration mode**   Router(config-line)#
- **Router configuration mode**   Router(config-router)#
- **IPX router configuration mode**   Router(config-ipx-router)#

Table 2-1 shows the most commonly used router configuration modes and how to navigate the user interface from one to another.

Examine the Router Status

From time to time, you will be called upon to examine the status of your routers—to see if a device is alive on the network, to verify the up/down status of an interface, or to determine what is causing the router to go into a slowdown. The commands we use to view the status of router elements and processes are known collectively as SHOW commands.

You will need to know the basic SHOW commands that allow you to view the elements we have just discussed. One of the more commonly used

TABLE 2-1	Common Command Modes		
Command Mode	**Access Method**	**Router Prompt**	**Exit Method**
User EXEC	Log in	Router>	Use the LOGOUT command.
Privileged EXEC	From user EXEC mode; enter the ENABLE command	Router#	To exit to user EXEC mode, use the DISABLE, EXIT, or LOGOUT command.
Global configuration	From the privileged EXEC mode, enter the CONFIGURE TERMINAL command	Router (config)#	To exit to the privileged EXEC mode, use the EXIT or END command; or press CTRL-Z.
Interface configuration	From the global configuration mode, enter the INTERFACE *type number* command, such as INTERFACE ETHERNET 0	Router (config-if)#	To exit to global configuration mode, use the EXIT command. To exit directly to the privileged EXEC mode press CTRL-Z.

SHOW commands is the SHOW INTERFACE command. Here is an example of this command and its result:

```
Router1#show interface tokenRing 1
TokenRing1 is up, line protocol is up
 Hardware is TMS380, address is 0000.303a.c2cd (bia 0000.303a.c2cd)
 Description: Lab Backbone
 Internet address is 172.16.1.1/26
 MTU 4464 bytes, BW 16000 Kbit, DLY 630 usec, rely 255/255, load 1/255
 Encapsulation SNAP, loopback not set, keepalive set (10 sec)
 ARP type: SNAP, ARP Timeout 04:00:00
 Ring speed: 16 Mbps
 Single ring node, Source Route Transparent Bridge capable
 Source bridging enabled, srn 2699 bn 1 trn 2710 (ring group)
   proxy explorers disabled, spanning explorer enabled, NetBIOS cache disabled
 Group Address: 0x00000000, Functional Address: 0x0880011A
Ethernet Transit OUI: 0x000000
Last input 00:00:00, output 00:00:01, output hang never
Last clearing of "show interface" counters never
Queueing strategy: fifo
Output queue 0/40, 0 drops; input queue 0/75, 0 drops
5 minute input rate 42000 bits/sec, 11 packets/sec
5 minute output rate 1000 bits/sec, 1 packets/sec
9868965 packets input, 3658968237 bytes, 0 no buffer
Received 7911721 broadcasts, 0 runts, 0 giants, 0 throttles
0 input errors, 0 CRC, 0 frame, 0 overrun, 0 ignored, 0 abort
2157045 packets output, 366298970 bytes, 0 underruns
0 output errors, 0 collisions, 0 interface resets
0 output buffer failures, 0 output buffers swapped out
0 transitions
```

The first line of this command is the one most often consulted to determine the status of an interface. There are two parts to this line. The first describes the status of the physical layer components, the second of the data link layer. An interface that is "up, up" is one that is fully operational. "TokenRing1 is up" means that the interface hardware has detected appropriate electrical signaling, or *carrier detect*. If there is no carrier signal, the interface will be down, and the line would read "TokenRing1 is down, line protocol is down."

The second part of this line, "line protocol is up," means that the router is detecting keepalive messages on the ring. It is possible for a carrier signal to be present, but no keepalive messages. In this case, the line would read, "TokenRing1 is up, line protocol is up."

If we wanted to turn off processing on this interface without physically connecting it to the network, we could put it in an *administratively down* status. If we had done this, the first line of output would read, "TokenRing1 is administratively down, line protocol is down."

Each type of physical interface, such as Ethernet or serial, has slightly different information in its SHOW INTERFACE display that is specific to that data-link technology.

Other SHOW commands that are useful include

- **SHOW RUNNING-CONFIG** Displays the router configuration currently running in RAM

- **SHOW STARTUP-CONFIG** Displays the router configuration stored in NVRAM. This is the configuration the router will use when it is powered on, unless specifically configured otherwise.

- **SHOW FLASH** Displays the formatting and contents of Flash memory, including the filename of the IOS image in Flash

- **SHOW BUFFERS** Displays statistics for the buffer pools on the router

- **SHOW MEMORY** Shows statistics about the router's memory, including free pool statistics

- **SHOW PROCESSES CPU** Displays statistics about the active processes, or programs, running in the router

- **SHOW PROTOCOLS** Shows information about all the protocols configured in the router and information about the network layer addresses configured on each of the interfaces

- **SHOW STACKS**   Displays information about the memory stack utilization of processes and interrupt routines, as well as the reason for the last system reboot

- **SHOW VERSION**   Displays the configuration of the system hardware, the software version, the names and sources of configuration files, and the boot images

Cisco Discovery Protocol

Cisco Discovery Protocol (CDP) is one of the best methods of understanding your network topology. CDP is a Layer 2 media- and protocol-independent protocol that runs on all Cisco-manufactured equipment, including routers, switches, and access servers. The devices do not need to have any network layer protocols configured in order to use CDP although, if these addresses are configured, CDP will discover them. Each device configured for CDP sends out periodic messages to a MAC layer multicast address. These advertisements include information about the capabilities and software version of the advertising platform. This gives you an easy way to see other Cisco devices on your network, without having to figure out which devices are Cisco by the vendor code embedded in the Media Access Control (MAC) address. Contents of the CDP table can be viewed with the following commands:

```
ROUTER1#show cdp neighbor
Capability Codes: R - Router, T - Trans Bridge, B - Source Route Bridge
                  S - Switch, H - Host, I - IGMP, r - Repeater
Device ID         Local Intrfce     Holdtme    Capability  Platform  Port ID
ROUTER3           Tok 0             143        R B         RSP4      Tok 0/0/0
ROUTER2           Ser 1             170        R           4700      Ser 1
ROUTER2           Ser 0             170        R           4700      Ser 0
```

This command shows information about Cisco devices locally attached to this device. *Locally attached* indicates that a device is either on the same

LAN segment or connected via a serial interface. Device ID is the host name of the advertising router. The Local Intrfce column indicates the interface on the router whose console you are at, and the "Port ID" column indicates the attached interface on the remote router.

CDP multicasts are normally sent every 30 seconds. The default holdtime is 180 seconds. The holdtime figure indicates how long this entry will continue in the router's CDP table if no more advertisements are heard from this neighbor.

```
ROUTER1#show cdp neighbor detail
-------------
Device ID: Router4
Entry address(es):
  IP address: 10.1.0.1
  Novell address: 0.0000.b010.0000
  DECnet address: 10.300
Platform: cisco 2509,  Capabilities: Router
Interface: Serial1,  Port ID (outgoing port): Serial0
Holdtime : 169 sec
Version :
Cisco Internetwork Operating System Software
IOS (tm) 2500 Software (C2500-JS40-L), Version 11.2(2), RELEASE SOFTWARE (fc1)
Copyright (c) 1986-1996 by cisco Systems, Inc.
Compiled Wed 13-Nov-96 02:07 by ajchopra
```

This command takes the previous command one step further. This command will show all network layer addresses of the advertising interface, as well as the IOS version. CDP is an excellent troubleshooting tool to determine neighboring devices that could be causing problems due to misconfigured addresses.

Remote Access to a Router

In a large network with many remote locations, it is impossible for a network administrator to gain physical console access to a router each time he or she needs to check its status or to change its configuration. It makes good sense to use the network itself to provide remote access to the routers in the network whenever possible. This is known as *in-band* management. Most often, the application used for remote access over an IP network is Telnet.

Every Cisco router has the Telnet application included in the IOS. This enables the administrator to establish a Telnet session into the router from any other IP host with Telnet capability, or to Telnet from the router itself to another router or IP host. You can perform most of the same configuration and status-checking functions from a Telnet session that you can perform from the router console.

Telnet sessions to or from the router are also called *virtual terminal* sessions. The router contains five virtual terminal lines (VTY lines) to accept incoming Telnet sessions. A Telnet session may be carried through any of the router's physical interfaces, and attach to any of the router's VTY lines.

In order for a router to accept an incoming Telnet session, at least one of its VTY lines must be configured with a password.

To initiate a Telnet session with a router, you must know an IP address of one of the interfaces in the router, or a symbolic name that can be resolved to an IP address in the router. The network must also be capable of routing the IP packets to that address; that is, the network portion of the address must be known to the routers in the internetwork that are between the host you are initiating the Telnet session from, and the target router.

The user interface presented by the Telnet application is identical to the interface at the router console, and is navigated in the same way.

Once you have established a Telnet session you may terminate it by entering the EXIT or QUIT commands. Sometimes, however, you know you will want to go back to that session, but you need to get back to the router you started from for a moment. If you want to suspend your session so you can go back to it within a short period of time, use the keystrokes CTRL-SHIFT-6-X. To get back to the suspended session, just press the ENTER key by itself on a line.

Basic Testing

The Cisco IOS software includes several commands that can be used to test basic connectivity in an IP network.

ping is a tool that tests connectivity at the network layer only. It operates by sending a series of ICMP echo packets to the destination, and keeping track of the ICMP echo-replies that the destination sends back. You may use ping with its default characteristics (five 100-byte packets, two-second timeout) from user EXEC mode; but, if you are in privileged EXEC mode, several other options become available to you. This is known as *extended ping*. Some of the other options available with extended ping include varying the sizes of the packets; increasing the timeout value; sending more than five packets at one time; setting the "don't fragment" bit in the IP header; and even using ping for other protocols, such as IPX and AppleTalk.

Here is sample output of a default ping. 172.20.2.1 is the IP address of our destination host.

```
Router1# ping 172.20.2.1
Type Escape sequence to abort.
Sending 5, 100-byte ICMP Echoes to 172.20.2.1, timeout is 2 seconds:
!!!!!
Success rate is 100 percent (5/5), round-trip min/avg/max = 1/15/64 ms
Router1#
```

The series of five exclamation points indicates the response packets received successfully by our router. A dot (period), instead of an exclamation point, indicates the request timed out, either because the ICMP echo request never reached its destination, or because the response was dropped or misrouted somewhere in the network.

Another command that tests network layer connectivity is the TRACEROUTE command. TRACEROUTE provides information about which path your traffic is taking through the internetwork, hop by hop, as well as how long each hop is taking. Here is an example of TRACEROUTE output:

```
Router1>trace 10.30.30.254
Type Escape sequence to abort.
Tracing the route to 10.30.30.254
  1 10.2.0.2 12 msec 12 msec 12 msec
  2 10.1.0.1 16 msec 12 msec 8 msec
  3 10.3.0.1 60 msec 56 msec *
Router1>
```

Debug

DEBUG is a tool you can use to get detailed diagnostic information from your router about routing processes and messages the router is receiving, sending, or acting upon. The debug privileged EXEC commands can provide a wealth of information about the traffic being seen (or not seen) on an interface, error messages generated by nodes on the network, protocol-specific diagnostic packets, and other useful troubleshooting data.

Great care should be taken when using the DEBUG command. By issuing a DEBUG command, you are asking the router to not only process traffic as normal, but to report information to the console or VTY session. The amount of processing power consumed by the DEBUG command varies with the quantity of information written to the console screen, which can vary dramatically according to the size and traffic load of the network. Some DEBUG commands generate a single line of output per packet, and others generate multiple lines of output per packet. Some generate large amounts of output, and others generate only occasional output. A DEBUG command that produces a large quantity of output can be very processor intensive, and may occupy so many of the routers processor cycles that it can cause network interruptions or even cause the router's operating system to freeze or crash.

The DEBUG command is issued from privileged EXEC mode and always requires arguments. You should use the context-sensitive Help feature to discover what they are for your particular IOS version and feature set. Always be as specific about the debug output as you can in order to avoid overburdening your router. You want the minimum volume of debug output that will give you the information you are seeking.

If you are using a VTY or Telnet session to the router, you will not see any debug output unless you use the command TERMINAL MONITOR. By default, debug output will only appear on the console screen.

Always remember to use the NO DEBUG or UNDEBUG ALL command to disable the debug output as soon as you are finished. See the following example of a debug output for an IGRP routing update being broadcast on several interfaces:

```
Router# debug ip igrp events
IGRP: sending update to 255.255.255.255 via Ethernet0 (172.16.1.1)
IGRP: Update contains 104 interior, 0 system, and 0 exterior routes.
IGRP: Total routes in update: 104
IGRP: Update contains 62 interior, 42 system, and 0 exterior routes.
IGRP: Total routes in update: 104
IGRP: Update contains 0 interior, 57 system, and 0 exterior routes.
IGRP: Total routes in update: 57
IGRP: sending update to 255.255.255.255 via TokenRing1 (172.17.1.1)
IGRP: Update contains 1 interior, 3 system, and 0 exterior routes.
IGRP: Total routes in update: 4
IGRP: sending update to 255.255.255.255 via TokenRing1 (192.168.23.10)
IGRP: Update contains 0 interior, 0 system, and 0 exterior routes.
IGRP: Total routes in update: 0 - suppressing null update
```

So, as you can see, DEBUG can be a very powerful tool to determine problems with your network. But keep in mind that you can cause serious network outages if you are not careful!

Routing Basics

Routers perform two basic functions: path determination and packet forwarding. The basic purpose of a router is to move information from one place to another. No matter what your protocol is—IP, IPX, AppleTalk, DECnet, or Vines—the purpose of the router does not change. It will perform the packet-forwarding function in the same way. When it receives a packet, it will consult its routing table for that protocol to find the next-hop address that will get the packet toward its destination, and it will forward the packet out of the interface toward that next hop.

A multiprotocol router maintains a separate routing table for each routed protocol. A routed protocol is a protocol that is used to carry user data, such as IPX or TCP/IP. A routing protocol is used only by the routers to tell each other what networks they know how to reach. A routing protocol is rarely used by host computers on a network. Routing protocols assist in the path-determination function by allowing the router to learn dynamically about the topology of the internetwork.

Path Determination

Routers use routing protocols to build and maintain routing tables and to forward data packets along the best path toward their destination networks. Routing protocols enable routers to learn about the status of networks that are not directly connected to them, and to communicate to other routers about the networks they are aware of. This communication is carried out on a continual basis, so the information in the routing table is updated as changes occur in the internetwork.

Routers that are neighbors on a link need to use the same routing protocol to communicate so that they can learn each other's routes and, in turn, communicate them to other neighboring routers. More than one routing protocol can be operational within a single router, although this is a practice you should avoid in designing your network, because it requires extreme care in the configuration.

The characteristics that distinguish one routing protocol from another include

- The routed protocol for which it maintains information
- The way the routers communicate among each other
- The frequency with which this communication takes place
- The algorithm and metrics used to determine the best path

There are two basic categories of routing protocols: distance vector and link-state.

Routers configured with a *distance-vector* protocol use frequent broadcasts of their entire routing tables on all their interfaces in order to communicate with neighboring routers. The more routes in their routing tables, the more routes that are broadcast. This limits the size of network that can use a distance-vector routing protocol efficiently. The *metric* (measure of preferability) of one link or path when compared to another is usually *hop count*. The hop count increases by one each time a packet must transit a router.

Look at Figure 2-1 to see how distance-vector protocols propagate routes through the network and build their routing tables. The routing tables contain identifiers for the individual networks, an interface within the router through which the router learned about that network, and the number of hops away the network is. C stands for "directly connected."

Notice that it takes two updates for all the routers to contain the same networks in their routing tables. When this has happened, the network is said to have *converged*. The time it takes for convergence to occur after a change in network topology is called *convergence time*.

The advantage of distance-vector protocols is their extreme simplicity. Hop count metrics are easy to administer, and the distance-vector protocols usually come with very few configurable parameters for tuning purposes.

The disadvantage is that hop count metrics make every link look the same, whether it is a 622-Mbps Sonet ring or a 1.544-Mbps T1 line.

Consider Figure 2-2. If we are using a classic distance-vector routing protocol to make our path determination for us, the lower path over the T1 link will look preferable, because it is only one hop. The upper path, even though the bandwidth is about 400 times as high, will not look as good, because it takes two hops to get from Router 1 to Router 2.

| FIGURE 2-1 | Routing table development in a distance-vector environment |

How routers learn each others' routes in a distance = vector network

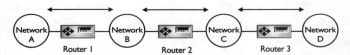

On power up, directly connected networks only are known, and the routing tables look like this:

A Int0 C	B Int0 C	C Int0 C
B Int1 C	C Int1 C	D Int1 C

After one update, networks one hop away are known, and the routing tables look like this:

A Int0 C	B Int0 C	C Int0 C
B Int1 C	C Int1 C	D Int1 C
C Int1 1	A Int0 1	B Int0 1
	D Int1 1	

After two updates, networks two hops away are known, and all routers know about the same routes. The network has converged:

A Int0 C	B Int0 C	C Int0 C
B Int1 C	C Int1 C	D Int1 C
C Int1 1	A Int0 1	B Int0 1
D Int1 2	D Int1 1	A Int0 2

FIGURE 2-2   Different metrics allow for different routing decisions

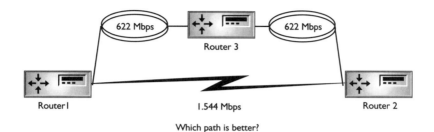

Which path is better?

It all depends on the *metrics* used by your routing protocol!

A *link-state routing protocol* can usually take bandwidth into account, because it uses a cost metric, which is inherently more sophisticated. Most cost metrics are based on factors such as bandwidth or delay. This enables the link-state protocol to make better routing decisions. It is also more efficient in terms of its bandwidth use for updates, because link-state protocols send out their updates only when a change occurs in the network.

Link-state protocols discover their neighboring routers by using a "hello" protocol, and they keep track of the updates and hellos received from their neighbors. Link-state updates are usually acknowledged, so there is no need to send out the same information again.

Convergence usually happens quickly in a link-state network, because updates are flooded immediately through the network and are sourced by the router directly connected to the link that has changed. There is no need for each router to wait for a periodic update to transmit the new information to its neighbor.

Forwarding

This process is basically the same for all protocols. In most cases, a host device (PC or server) determines that it must send a packet to another host. Having acquired a gateway router's address by some means, the source host sends a packet addressed specifically to a router's physical MAC layer address, but with the protocol (network layer) address of the destination host.

On examining the packet's destination protocol address (as you recall, Layer 3) the router determines that it either knows or does not know how to forward the packet to the next hop. If the router does not know how to forward the packet, it will drop the packet. If the router knows how to forward the packet, it changes the destination physical address to that of the next hop and transmits the packet.

The next hop may or may not be the ultimate destination host. If not, the next hop is usually another router, which executes the same switching decision process. As the packet moves through the internetwork, its physical address changes but its protocol address remains constant

Once a packet is routed to the destination, it must be placed on the LAN segment for which it was intended. The router at that point will repeat the same process as the host did before the packet was sent. The router will determine the destination host's MAC layer address. The router will then place that host's MAC address on the packet and forward it.

The key is that no matter what your routed protocol is, or what your routing protocol is, the routers each make independent forwarding decisions based on the routing information stored in their routing tables. The routers forward packets on a hop-by-hop basis, one step at a time.

CERTIFICATION OBJECTIVE 2.03

Initial Configuration

When you power up your router, it first needs to test its hardware, including memory and interfaces. The next step in the sequence is to find and load an IOS image—the operating system for the router. Finally, before the router can function properly in your network, it needs to find its configuration information and apply it.

If you are at the router console when it is powered on you should see something similar to the following:

```
System Bootstrap, Version 5.1(1) [daveu 1], RELEASE SOFTWARE (fc1)
Copyright (c) 1994 by cisco Systems, Inc.
C4500 processor with 32768 Kbytes of main memory
```

At this point, the router has loaded the bootstrap program from ROM. Next, it will load its IOS image from Flash. It first verifies the file integrity, then decompresses the image as it loads into RAM. These processes are represented by Rs and #s.

```
Booting yj11120n from flash memory RRRRRRRRRRRRRRRRRRRRRRRRRRRRRRRRRRRRRRRR
RRRRRRRRRRRRRRRRRRRRRRRRRRRRRRRRRRRRRRRRRRRRRRRRRRRRRRRRRRRRRRRRRRRRRRRRRRRRRRRR
RRRRRRRRRRRRRRRRRRRRRRRRRRRRRRRRRRRRRRRRRRRRRRRRRRRRRRRRRRRRRRRRRRRRRRRRRRRRRRRR
RRRRRRRRRRRRRRRRRRRRRRRRRRRRRRRRRRRRRRRRRRRRRR
[OK - 1337256/3532618 bytes]
########################################################################
########################################################################
########################################################################
#######################################
F3: 1926336+46904+183152 at 0x12000
```

Next we see some copyright notices and other information about the software and its features.

```
Restricted Rights Legend
Use, duplication, or disclosure by the Government is
subject to restrictions as set forth in subparagraph
(c) of the Commercial Computer Software - Restricted
Rights clause at FAR sec. 52.227-19 and subparagraph
(c) (1) (ii) of the Rights in Technical Data and Computer
Software clause at DFARS sec. 252.227-7013.
cisco Systems, Inc.
170 West Tasman Drive
San Jose, California 94134-1706
Cisco Internetwork Operating System Software
IOS (tm) 4500 Software (C4500-AJ-M), Version 11.1(2)
Copyright (c) 1986-1996 by cisco Systems, Inc.
Compiled Mon 24-May-96 22:46 [mikehub 107]
cisco 4500 (R4K) processor (revision 0x00) with 32768K/4096K bytes of memory.
Processor ID 01242622
R4600 processor, Implementation 32, Revision 1.0
G.703/E1 software, Version 1.0
Bridging software.
SuperLAT software (copyright 1990 by Meridian Technology Corp).
X.25 software, Version 2.0, NET2, BFE and GOSIP compliant.
TN3270 Emulation software (copyright 1994 by TGV Inc.).
```

FROM THE CLASSROOM

A Perspective on Passwords

It is easy for students to be confused about how passwords are used in the Cisco routers and what the implications are for setting or not setting them.

Your router needs at least four passwords set for minimal security: an enable password, a console password, an auxiliary line password, and a VTY password. Unless you have configured the router to refer to a separate authentication server for this function, passwords are stored in the router's configuration file. They can be encrypted or stored in clear text, depending on your security environment.

The primary password for router security is the enable password. This password controls access to privileged mode in your router, which allows the user to make configuration changes and do testing that could potentially disrupt network operations. By default, the enable password is not encrypted as it is stored in the configuration file.

You may have noticed in the section on the setup dialog that you are prompted for an "enable secret." The enable secret, if you have set one, overrides the enable password, and is always stored encrypted in the router's configuration. So if you have set an enable secret, the enable password will not be used

unless your router boots from an old software version (possibly stored in ROM or on a network TFTP server) that does not recognize the enable secret. It is considered a bad idea to set the enable password the same as the enable secret. This eliminates the very security benefit the enable secret is designed to provide.

By default, the router requires that passwords be set on the VTY lines in order to use them for incoming Telnet sessions. If you don't set a password on your VTY lines and try to Telnet into the router, you will get an error message, "password required but none set." If you need those Telnet sessions for remote management, be sure to set a VTY password! If you are working in a lab environment and don't want to type in a password each time you Telnet to a router, remove the "login" command under the VTY line configuration. This will eliminate the requirement for this password.

The default router configuration does not require passwords on the auxiliary or console lines. If you want to require passwords on these lines, you must not only set a password on them but also configure a "login" command on them. Without the "login" command, the password prompt will not appear and your password will be ignored.

FROM THE CLASSROOM

In a lab or classroom environment you may choose not to set an enable password (or enable secret), but that isn't a good idea. If you don't set an enable password (or enable secret), the only connection from which you can get into privileged mode will be the console. That means that if you try to connect through the aux port or through a Telnet session, you won't have any access to privileged mode if you haven't set that enable password. There are situations in which you can be essentially locked out of the router without this password set—it has happened to me.

Cisco offers an encryption service for those passwords that normally would appear in clear text in the configuration file (not the enable secret). You can turn this on at the console by using the command SERVICE PASSWORD-ENCRYPTION. Once you enter this command, each password you configure will

be stored in encrypted form and cannot be recovered without a password-cracking program. This is useful if your configuration files are stored on a TFTP server; it will prevent a casual observer from determining your router passwords. It is not considered to be strong encryption, however, and will not discourage a determined hacker who wishes to break into your network.

Cisco uses the MD5 algorithm to encrypt the enable secret. There is no known way to reverse this algorithm. If you use the enable secret you will not be able to use the normal techniques for password recovery, which depend on viewing the password in clear text within the startup configuration file. You will need to reset the password, because there is no way to recover it.

—*By Pamela Forsyth, CCIE, CCSI, CNX*

Next, the router inventories and tests its interfaces. Because most of the Cisco routers come in a variety of hardware configurations, the software must be able to detect what particular interfaces are present in the router when it powers up.

```
2 Ethernet/IEEE 802.3 interfaces.
2 Token Ring/IEEE 802.5 interfaces.
4 ISDN Basic Rate interfaces.
2 Serial network interfaces.
128K bytes of non-volatile configuration memory.
8192K bytes of processor board System Flash (Read/Write)
4096K bytes of processor board Boot Flash (Read/Write)
Notice: NVRAM invalid, possibly due to write erase.
-- System Configuration Dialog --
At any point you may enter a question mark '?' for help.
Refer to the 'Getting Started' Guide for additional help.
Use CTRL-c to abort configuration dialog at any prompt.
Default settings are in square brackets '[]'.
Would you like to enter the initial configuration dialog? [yes]:
```

If the router does not find a configuration file in NVRAM and is not configured to look for one on the network, it will begin the setup dialog. The nice thing is that this is menu driven; all you have to do is answer the questions. When you are asked, "Would you like to enter the initial configuration dialog?," if you answer **no**, you will enter the normal operating mode. A **yes** answer will take you through the menu.

The setup dialog allows you to get your router running with a very basic configuration. It will allow you to name your router, set an enable password and enable secret, enable any of the network layer protocols and assign appropriate addresses to router interfaces, and enable dynamic routing protocols. You will want to check the configuration file produced by this process in order to refine the configuration.

Virtual Configuration Register Settings

Every Cisco router has a 16-bit configuration register, that is stored in a special memory location in NVRAM. This register controls a number of functions, some of which are listed here:

■ Force the system into the bootstrap program

- Select a boot source and default boot filename
- Enable or disable the console Break function
- Set the console terminal baud rate
- Load operating software from ROM
- Enable booting from a TFTP server

The configuration register boot field is the portion of the configuration register that determines whether the router loads an IOS image and, if so, where to get this image from. The least significant four bits, bits 0 through 3, of the configuration register make up the boot field.

If the boot field value is 0x0 (all four bits set to zeros), the router will enter ROM monitor mode.

If the boot field value is 0x1 (binary 0001), the router will boot from the image in ROM.

If the boot field value is 0x2 through 0xF (binary 0010 through 1111), the router will follow the normal boot sequence and will look for boot system commands in the configuration file in NVRAM.

Enter the SHOW VERSION EXEC command to display the configuration register value currently in effect, and the value that will be used at the next reload. The value will be displayed on the last line of the screen display, as in the following example:

```
ROUTER1#show version
Cisco Internetwork Operating System Software
IOS (tm) 4500 Software (C4500-JS-M), Version 11.2(7a)P, SHARED PLATFORM, RELEASE
SOFTWARE (fc1)
Copyright (c) 1986-1997 by cisco Systems, Inc.
Compiled Wed 02-Jul-97 05:32 by ccai
Image text-base: 0x60008900, data-base: 0x60820000
ROM: System Bootstrap, Version 5.3(16) [richardd 16], RELEASE SOFTWARE (fc1)
BOOTFLASH: 4500 Software (C4500-BOOT-M), Version 11.1(7), RELEASE SOFTWARE (fc2)
ROUTER1 uptime is 12 weeks, 6 days, 10 hours, 30 minutes
System restarted by power-on at 01:09:36 Central Sun Apr 5 1998
System image file is "flash:c4500-js-mz.112-7a.P", booted via flash
```

```
Network configuration file is "pcmdiAAAa006h_162", booted via tftp from 172.16.1.1
cisco 4700 (R4K) processor (revision F) with 32768K/4096K bytes of memory.
Processor board ID 06755819
R4700 processor, Implementation 33, Revision 1.0 (512KB Level 2 Cache)
G.703/E1 software, Version 1.0.
Bridging software.
SuperLAT software (copyright 1990 by Meridian Technology Corp).
X.25 software, Version 2.0, NET2, BFE and GOSIP compliant.
TN3270 Emulation software.
2 Token Ring/IEEE 802.5 interface(s)
4 Serial network interface(s)
128K bytes of non-volatile configuration memory.
8192K bytes of processor board System flash (Read/Write)
4096K bytes of processor board Boot flash (Read/Write)
Configuration register is 0x142 (will be 0x102 at next reload)
```

Startup Sequence—Boot System Commands

You can place special commands in the router's configuration file that will instruct it where to look for its IOS image. The router will scan these entries and try to execute them in sequence when it boots up. This provides you with several fallback options in case the router's flash memory becomes corrupted. These are called boot system commands.

Usually you will want the router to boot from flash memory. The boot system command for this is

```
Router1(config)# boot system flash
```

If you do not specify a filename, the router loads the first valid file it finds in flash memory.

In most cases, you will want the router to find a backup IOS image on a TFTP server somewhere in your network if it cannot find and load an image from Flash memory. The command to designate this is

```
Router1(config)# boot system tftp 172.16.1.150
```

You may wish to have more than one TFTP server on your network that stores your backup IOS images. You may have as many boot system TFTP commands as you like in your router configuration for redundancy.

```
Router1(config)# boot system rom
```

This command boots the router from ROM. This is a last resort, just to get the router running so you can diagnose the problem. The system image in ROM will not have as many features and capabilities as the full IOS version in Flash, so your router may not operate in a predictable way if it boots from ROM.

Be very careful of the order in which these commands are entered into the router. For best results, you will need to enter THE BOOT SYSTEM FLASH prior to the BOOT SYSTEM ROM. If the ROM command is entered prior to the FLASH command, the router will reload IOS from ROM and not from Flash. That boot system ROM command is very useful to ensure that if the Flash image is corrupted in any way, the router will come back online—in a limited mode, but back online—to allow you to download another IOS image.

Configuring to/from a TFTP Server

The router also has the capability to copy its configuration to and from a TFTP server. This gives the network administrator the ability to store configurations out to a server for configuration tracking, change auditing, or distress recovery. You will need to store your configuration on a TFTP server if it is larger than 32,000 bytes, which is the largest configuration that can fit into NVRAM. When you TFTP a configuration to the router, you can place it in Flash, NVRAM, or RAM memory. When you place the configuration into Flash, you will still need to place it into NVRAM or RAM in order for the router to be able to use it. The COPY TFTP commands can be done via either the console or a VTY session.

The commands for copying configuration files to and from TFTP servers are as follows:

- **COPY TFTP RUNNING-CONFIG** Configures the router directly from the TFTP server by copying into the configuration in RAM

- **COPY TFTP STARTUP-CONFIG** Overwrites the configuration file stored in NVRAM with the file from the TFTP server

- **COPY RUNNING-CONFIG TFTP** Makes a copy of the router's running configuration in RAM on the TFTP server

- **COPY STARTUP-CONFIG TFTP** Copies the configuration stored in NVRAM to the TFTP server

Before you try to TFTP your configuration, be sure to verify that you can reach your TFTP server. It's not going to do you much good to try and TFTP a file to or from a server that is offline. The PING command is useful for verifying that your TFTP server can communicate with your router.

If the ping fails, verify that you have the correct IP address for the server and that the server is active (powered on), and repeat the PING command. Always remember to back up your work! Prior to downloading a new IOS or configuration file, copy the existing one in the router to the TFTP server. It is also a good idea to go to the TFTP server (or Telnet to it) and verify the exact filename as it exists on the server.

You may also change or upgrade your router's IOS image by copying a new file from a TFTP server, or back up your router's current image by copying it to a TFTP server. The following output shows the process of copying an IOS image from the router's Flash memory to a TFTP server.

```
Router1# copy flash tftp c4500-js-mz.111-17a.P
IP address of remote host [255.255.255.255]? 172.20.2.1
Name of file to copy []? c4500-js-mz.111-17a.P
writing c4500-js-mz.111-17a.P
!!!!!!!!!!!!!!!!!!!!!!!!!!!!!!!!!!!!!!!!!!!!!!!!!!!!!!!!
Router1#
```

You may also copy an IOS image from a TFTP server into the router's flash memory. This is accomplished by the command COPY TFTP FLASH.

```
Router1(config)#copy tftp flash
File name/status c4500-js-mz.111-17a.P
 [123816/2097152 bytes free/total
IP address or name of remote host [255.255.255.255]? 172.20.2.1
Name of file to copy ? c4500-js-mz.112-7a.P
Copy c4500-js-mz.112-7a.P from 172.20.2.1 into Flash address space ?
[confirm]<Return>
123752 bytes available for writing without erasure.
Erase Flash address space before writing? [confirm] <Return>
bank 0...zzzzzzzzzzzzzzzzzvvvvvvvvvvvvvvvvvveeeeeeeeeeeeeeee
bank 1...zzzzzzzzzzzzzzzzzvvvvvvvvvvvvvvvvvveeeeeeeeeeeeeeee
Loading from 172.20.2.1: !!!!!!!!!!!!!!!!!!!!!!!!!!!!!!!!!!!!!!!!!!!!!!!!!!!
!!!!!!!!!!!!!!!!!!!!!!!!!!!!!!!!!!!!!!!!!!!!!!!!!!!!!!!!!!!!!!!!!!!!!!!!!!!!!!!
!!!!!!!!!!!!!!!!!!!!!!!!!!!!!!!!!!!!!!!!!!!!!!!!!!!!!!!!!!!!!!!!!!!!!!!!!!!!!!!
!!!!!!!!!!!!!!!!!!!!!!!!!!!!!!!!!!!!!!!!!!!!!!!!! [OK - 1337256/2097088 bytes]
Verify checksum...vvvvvvvvvvvvvvvvvvvvvVerification successful:
 Length = 1337256, checksum = 0x5A1C
```

You are prompted for the filename of the image you want to copy. This name is case sensitive, so it pays to verify the exact name on the TFTP server. You will then be prompted for the IP address of the TFTP server. The router will verify the amount of free space in Flash memory and will ask you if you want to erase the existing file in Flash before copying the new one. Once Flash is erased, the router will load the new file from the TFTP server. Each exclamation point in the display signifies a block of the file successfully loaded. Finally, the router will verify the integrity of the complete file.

Caution: do not make any typographical errors using the COPY TFTP FLASH command when you specify the filename of the system software image you are copying. If you type a filename that does not exist when using the COPY TFTP FLASH command, then tell the system to erase the current image, the router erases the existing image in Flash memory. If this happens, the router still has a working image in RAM, so your router will still function. If you think you have tried to load a nonexistent file, do not reboot the router! If you do, your router will not have a functional image in Flash memory. To recover from the accidental Flash memory erasure, execute the COPY TFTP FLASH command again to load the appropriate image into Flash memory.

CERTIFICATION OBJECTIVE 2.04

AutoInstalling Configuration Data

The AutoInstall process is designed to configure the router automatically after connection to your wide-area network (WAN). For AutoInstall to work properly, a Transmission Control Protocol/Internet Protocol (TCP/IP) host on your network must be running as a TFTP server, and preconfigured to provide the required configuration files. The TCP/IP host can exist anywhere on the network, as long as the following two conditions are maintained:

- The host must be on the remote side of the router's synchronous serial connection to the WAN.
- User Datagram Protocol (UDP) broadcasts to and from the router and the TCP/IP host must be enabled.

Your system administrator at the site where the TCP/IP host is located coordinates this functionality. You should not attempt to use AutoInstall unless the required files have been provided on the TCP/IP host. See the appropriate software configuration publications for information on how AutoInstall works.

Use the following procedure to prepare your router for the AutoInstall process:

1. Attach the appropriate synchronous serial cable to a synchronous serial interface on the router.

2. Turn on power to the router.

The router will load the operating system image from Flash memory. If the remote end of the WAN connection is connected and properly configured, the AutoInstall process will begin.

If the AutoInstall process completes successfully, you might want to write the configuration data to the router's NVRAM. Perform the following step to complete this task:

3. At the # prompt, enter the COPY RUNNING-CONFIG STARTUP-CONFIG command if you are running Cisco IOS Release 11.0 or above, or the WRITE MEMORY command if you are running a Cisco IOS release earlier than 11.0:

   Hostname# copy running-config startup-config

Taking this step saves the configuration settings that the AutoInstall process created in the router. If you fail to do this, your configuration will be lost the next time you reload the router.

CERTIFICATION SUMMARY

The Cisco router's user interface is a command-line interface. Router modes limit and organize the commands that are available to the user. The lowest level of access to the router is user EXEC mode, in which the user can verify router status and perform basic troubleshooting. The highest level of access is privileged EXEC mode, in which the user can change the router's configuration and perform extensive network testing and diagnostics. The command to enter privileged EXEC mode is ENABLE. Context-sensitive Help and advanced editing features facilitate configuration and verification tasks.

The router's configurable elements include memory (RAM, ROM, Flash, and NVRAM), interfaces for connecting to networks, and ports for user access and configuration. SHOW commands allow the user to verify the status or view the contents of these elements in an operational router.

Router modes allowing for configuration changes include global configuration mode, interface configuration mode, line configuration mode, and router configuration mode.

Cisco Discovery Protocol (CDP) allows Cisco devices to discover each other in the network regardless of whether they have network layer protocols configured. Telnet can be used to gain remote access to routers over the network. ping and traceroute are useful to test network layer connectivity. Debug allows the user to get detailed information about almost every aspect of the router's operation, although it must be used with great care to prevent overburdening the router.

Dynamic routing protocols can be categorized as either distance-vector or link-state. Distance-vector routers broadcast their entire routing tables periodically to each other. Link-state routers keep track of their neighbors, and flood updates through the network only when changes occur. Convergence is a state in which all routers in the network have a consistent view of the network topology.

When a router first powers up, it tests its hardware, locates and loads an IOS image, and applies configuration information. The startup sequence is controlled by the lowest four bits in the configuration register—the boot field. The boot field is used in conjunction with boot system commands in the configuration file to tell the router where to find its configuration information and its IOS image.

If a router does not find a valid configuration file when it boots up, it will enter the setup dialog. The setup dialog can be used to create a basic configuration for your router.

In a WAN environment, a new router can get its configuration information automatically from a TFTP server on the network. This facilitates configuration of routers at remote sites.

 ## TWO-MINUTE DRILL

- ❑ The most common way to interact with the router is through the command-line interface provided by the Cisco IOS software.
- ❑ In order to begin working with the router from the console, you will need to log in.
- ❑ The highest level of access to the router is *privileged EXEC mode*, sometimes called enable mode, because the command you use to get into this mode is ENABLE.
- ❑ To leave privileged EXEC mode and revert to user EXEC mode, use the command DISABLE.

❑ To log out of the router entirely and end your console session, use the command EXIT or LOGOUT.

❑ If you want to know all the commands available to you at any time, just enter a question mark (?) at the prompt.

❑ Many commands you will be using have many parts or *arguments*.

❑ The hardware components of the router include memory, processor, lines, and interfaces.

❑ The whole point of a router is to forward packets from one network to another.

❑ Some of the most common router interfaces are serial (which generally connect the router to wide-area links) and the LAN interfaces: Ethernet, Token Ring, and FDDI.

❑ The router's command executive has a hierarchy of modes that limit and organize the commands available to you, the user, as you configure the router.

❑ Once you are in privileged EXEC mode, you may enter *global configuration mode*.

❑ The commands we use to view the status of router elements and processes are known collectively as SHOW commands.

❑ Each type of physical interface, such as Ethernet or serial, has slightly different information in its SHOW INTERFACE display that is specific to that data-link technology.

❑ Cisco Discovery Protocol (CDP) is one of the best methods of understanding your network topology. CDP is a Layer 2 media- and protocol-independent protocol that runs on all Cisco-manufactured equipment, including routers, switches, and access servers.

❑ In a large network with many remote locations, it is impossible for a network administrator to gain physical console access to a router each time he or she needs to check its status or change its configuration. This is known as *in-band* management.

❑ Every Cisco router has the Telnet application included in the IOS.

❑ In order for a router to accept an incoming Telnet session, at least one of its VTY lines must be configured with a password.

❑ The Cisco IOS software includes several commands that can be used to test basic connectivity in an IP network.

❑ *ping* is a tool that tests connectivity at the network layer only.

❑ TRACEROUTE provides information about which path your traffic is taking through the internetwork, hop by hop, as well as how long each hop is taking.

❑ DEBUG is a tool you can use to get detailed diagnostic information from your router about routing processes and messages the router is receiving, sending, or acting upon.

❑ Routers perform two basic functions: path determination and packet forwarding.

❑ When you power up your router, it first needs to test its hardware, including memory and interfaces.

❑ Every Cisco router has a 16-bit configuration register, which is stored in a special memory location in NVRAM.

❑ You can place special commands in the router's configuration file that will instruct it where to look for its IOS image.

❑ The router also has the capability to copy its configuration to and from a TFTP server.

❑ The AutoInstall process is designed to configure the router automatically after connection to your wide-area network (WAN).

SELF TEST

The following Self-Test questions will help you measure your understanding of the material presented in this chapter. Read all the choices carefully, as there may be more than one correct answer. Choose all correct answers for each question.

1. What command would you use to log out of the router and end your session? (Select two.)

   A. TERMINATE

   B. logout

   C. exit

   D. session end

2. If you type a command that the router doesn't recognize, what will the router do?

   A. Display an error message.

   B. Try to resolve the command to an IP address.

   C. Try to execute the closest command it can find in its command set.

   D. Invalidate the configuration.

3. You can confirm that you are in the privileged EXEC mode by which prompt?

   A. Router>

   B. Router(config)#

   C. Router#

   D. Router(config-if)#

4. A reload of the router is required to get the configuration changes to take place.

   A. True

   B. False

5. By default, how many commands are stored in the command history buffer?

   A. 5

   B. 10

   C. 15

   D. 20

6. The IOS image is normally stored in?

   A. RAM

   B. NVRAM

   C. Shared

   D. Flash

7. The startup configuration file is stored in NVRAM.

   A. True

   B. False

8. To determine the operational status of an interface, which command do you use?

   A. DISPLAY INTERFACE STATUS

   B. show interface

   C. show status interface

   D. display interface

9. The boot field consists of:

   A. The lowest four bits of the configuration register

   B. The same as the configuration register

   C. The highest four bits of the configuration register

   D. Bits 4 through 7 of the configuration register

10. A boot field value of 0x1 will cause the router to

   A. Boot from Flash.

   B. Look for boot system commands in the startup configuration.

   C. Look for an IOS image on a TFTP server.

   D. Boot from ROM.

11. To view the configuration register settings, which command do you enter?

   A. SHOW RUNNING-CONFIGURATION

   B. show startup-configuration

   C. show version

   D. show controllers

12. What command is required to send Debug output to a VTY session?

   A. SHOW DEBUG

   B. show log

   C. terminal monitor

   D. debug all

13. Which keystroke would you use to recall the previous command in the command history buffer?

   A. CTRL-N

   B. CTRL-P

   C. ESC-P

   D. ESC-F

14. You must have an IP address assigned to an interface in order for CDP to operate.

   A. True

   B. False

15. What is the command to view the stored configuration in NVRAM?

   A. SHOW RUNNING-CONFIG

   B. show startup-config

   C. show version

   D. show NVRAM

16. When do configuration commands take effect?

   A. When you reload the router

   B. When they are saved in NVRAM

   C. As soon as you press the ENTER key

   D. When you enter the command ENABLE

17. What command is needed to see if an interface is up and operational?

   A. SHOW CONTROLLERS

   B. show running-config

   C. show interface

   D. show buffers

18. What is the best command to enter to determine which release of IOS the router is running?

   A. SHOW FLASH

   B. show running-config

   C. show startup-config

   D. show version

19. What is the command needed to copy the current operational configuration to a TFTP server?

    A. COPY RUNNING-CONFIG TFTP

    B. copy startup-config tftp

    C. copy tftp running-config

    D. copy tftp startup-config

20. What command would you use to see information about all the protocols enabled in the router?

    A. DISPLAY PROTOCOL INFORMATION

    B. display protocols

    C. show protocol route

    D. show protocols

21. What is the part of the IOS software that provides the user interface and interprets the commands you type?

    A. The virtual terminal

    B. The command executive

    C. The console port

    D. The configuration register

22. What command allows you to view the configuration in RAM?

    A. SHOW STARTUP-CONFIG

    B. show RAM-config

    C. show running-config

    D. show config

23. Which of the following represents access via a physical connection of a terminal to a router?

    A. Virtual terminal

    B. IOS

    C. Console

    D. All of the above

24. What command would you use to view the name of the filename in Flash memory?

    A. SHOW MEMORY ALL

    B. show flash

    C. show filename

    D. show flash partitions

25. What is the level of access to the router in which you are allowed to change the router's configuration?

    A. User EXEC mode

    B. High-level access mode

    C. Privileged EXEC mode

    D. Console mode

26. Changes to the router configuration are allowed from the user EXEC mode.

    A. True

    B. False

27. How can you confirm you are in privileged EXEC mode?

    A. By issuing the command CONFIRM MODE

    B. By viewing the output of the SHOW VERSION command

    C. By noting the router's prompt

    D. None of the above

28. After giving the command INTERFACE ETHERNET0 from global configuration mode, the router is most likely to respond with

    A. router(config)#

    B. router#interface

    C. router(config-if)#

    D. router#(config-int)

29. To completely get out of the interface configuration mode and back to privileged EXEC mode, what should you use?

    A. CTRL-Z

    B. EXIT

    C. END CONFIG

    D. LOGOUT

30. The response to the command ROUTER# CONFIGURE ? will be

    A. Connect, copy, configure

    B. Various paths from source to destination

    C. router(config)#

    D. A list of possible options from where the router can be configured

31. Which are the types of memory elements in a Cisco router?

    A. RAM, ROM, NVRAM, and Boot

    B. RAM, ROM, NVRAM, and Flash

    C. Config, RAM, ROM, NVRAM, and Flash

    D. Buffers, RAM, NVRAM, and Flash

32. How do you suspend a Telnet session?

    A. Use the command SUSPEND SESSION.

    B. Use the keystrokes CTRL-ALT-6.

    C. Use the keystrokes CTRL-SHIFT-6-X .

    D. A Telnet session cannot be suspended. You must quit the session and initiate it again if you want to go back to it.

33. What is the characteristic of a link-state routing protocol that enables it to make better routing decisions?

    A. Its metrics take bandwidth into account.

    B. It uses a hello protocol.

    C. It broadcasts the contents of its routing table periodically to its neighbors.

    D. None of the above.

34. What is the sequence of events that occurs when you power up your router?

    A. Find configuration file, load IOS image, test hardware

    B. Load IOS image, test hardware, find configuration file

    C. Test hardware, find configuration file, load IOS image

    D. Test hardware, load IOS image, find configuration file

35. The size of the configuration register is

    A. 16 bits

    B. 12 bits

    C. 8 bits

    D. 4 bits

36. It is recommended that, in order to obtain best results, the BOOT SYSTEM FLASH command be entered after the BOOT SYSTEM ROM command.

    A. True

    B. False

37. The command routerx(config)#boot system tftp 189.12.3.172
    will boot the router from

    A. System image in Flash

    B. System image 189.12.3.172 from RAM

    C. System image 189.12.3.172 from TFTP

    D. System image from TFTP

38. A good connection is indicated by which of the following in an output display of the PING command?

    A. !!!!!

    B. .....

    C. xxxxx

    D. ******

39. If a mistake is made in specifying the file name in the COPY TFTP FLASH command, the router will still function because

    A. It still has working image in ROM.

    B. It still has working image in RAM.

    C. It still has working image in Flash.

    D. It still has working image in TFTP.

40. The command COPY FLASH TFTP FILE2600 copies

    A. Contents of file from Flash into file2600 of the TFTP server

    B. Contents of TFTP into file2600 in the Flash

    C. Contents of file2600 in the TFTP to file2600 in the Flash

    D. Contents of file2600 in the TFTP into Flash

41. What command can be used to see the router's neighbors from your local router if no network layer protocols are configured?

    A. SHOW CDP

    B. show cdp neighbor

    C. show neighbor

    D. show network

42. In order to show the neighbor's IOS version, what optional parameter can be used in the command SHOW CDP NEIGHBOR?

    A. VERSION

    B. IOS

    C. detail

    D. None of the above

43. In a Cisco router, configuration register information can be used to

    A. Select a boot source and default file name.

    B. Enable booting from a TFTP server.

    C. Load operating software from ROM.

    D. All of the above.

3

IP Addressing

The specifications for the Internet Protocol (IP) were established by RFC 791 in 1982. Part of these specifications outlined a structure for IP addresses. This structure provides for a 32-bit logical address for each host and router interface. An IP address is expressed as four decimal values in the range of 0–255, separated by periods. These decimal values each represent eight bits of the 32-bit address, known as an *octet*. This is called *dotted decimal* notation. An example of this would be 155.127.23.12.

The IP protocol is used for end-to-end routing of data across a network, which may mean that an IP packet must travel across multiple networks, and may cross several router interfaces to get to its destination. At the IP level, the destination IP address remains the same, but since each interface may have its own hardware address, the packet's destination hardware address changes as it crosses each interface on the way to the destination. The constant IP destination address forms the basis for routing the packet through the network to its final destination.

This chapter will cover the basics of IP addressing, including issues such as address structure and classes, and the role of subnet masks. It will also describe the process of segmenting a network into subnets through the use of subnet masks. Finally, it will explain the command syntax used by Cisco IOS to configure IP addressing on a router.

When you have completed this chapter, you will be able to

- Explain the use and implementation of IP address classes.
- Explain subnetting and the use of subnet masks.
- Describe the process of subnet planning.
- Describe some complex subnetting techniques.
- Describe IP address configuration and testing commands on a Cisco router.

CERTIFICATION OBJECTIVE 3.01

Classes of IP Addresses

As originally defined, the IP addressing standard did not provide for address classes; these were later added to provide ease of administration. The implementation of address classes divided the address space into a limited number of very large networks (Class A), a much larger number of intermediate-sized networks (Class B), and a very large number of small networks (Class C). In addition, some special address classes were also defined, including Class D (used for multicasting), and Class E, which is generally referred to as the experimental or research class. Although there are exceptions to the rules expressed here, the focus of this chapter will be on *classful* IP addressing.

Structure of an IP Address

The 32-bit structure of an IP address is comprised of both a network address and a host address. The number of bits assigned to each of these components varies with the address class. The scheme employed in IP addressing is roughly analogous to the concept of a street address. Just as a house may be defined as being at 121 Main St., an IP address includes the network address (Main St.), as well as the host address (number 121). Our house address makes it possible for the mail to reach our house, and an IP address makes it possible to route data from a source host to its destination.

Figure 3-1 depicts the organization of network addresses using a network and host address.

The concept of *subnetting* extends the network portion of the address to allow a single network to be divided into a number of logical sections (subnets). Routers look at each of these subnets as distinct networks, and can

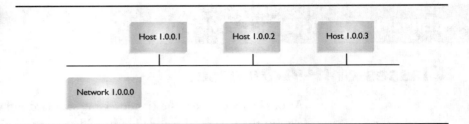

Network and host
addresses

route among them. This helps in managing large networks, as well as isolating
traffic between different portions of the network. This traffic isolation is possible
because network hosts, by default, can only communicate with other hosts on
the same network. In order to communicate with other networks, we need to
use a router. A router is essentially a computer with multiple interfaces. Each
interface is attached to a different network or subnet. Software within the router
performs the function of relaying traffic between networks or subnets. To do
this, it accepts packets via an interface with an address on the source network,
and relays it through an interface attached to the destination network, as
illustrated in Figure 3-2.

By using a router, only traffic that needs to traverse a network other than
its local network will pass the router boundary. If the network is designed so
that hosts routinely communicate within their own subnets, and only cross
the router on an exception basis, the network can handle much more traffic
than it could if it were not segmented.

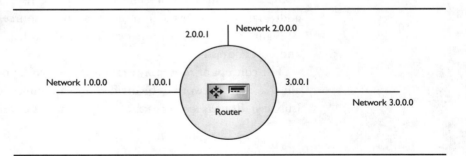

Router among networks
showing router interface
addresses

Special Cases: Loopback, Broadcast, and Network Addresses

Certain addresses in the IP address space have been reserved for special purposes, and are not normally allowed as host addresses. The rules for these reserved addresses are as follows:

- The network address portion of an IP address cannot be set to "all binary 1's" or "all binary 0's"

- The subnet portion of an IP address cannot be set to "all binary 1's" or "all binary 0's"

- The host address portion of an IP address cannot be set to "all binary 1's" or all binary 0's"

- The network 127.*x.x.x* cannot be used as a network address

Network Addresses

When all the bits in the host portion of an IP address are set to zero, it indicates the network, rather than a specific host on that network. These types of entries are often found in routing tables, since routers control traffic between networks, not individual hosts.

In a subnetted network, setting the host bits to 0 would indicate the specific subnet. Also, the bits allocated for the subnet may not be all 0's, since this would refer to the network address of the parent network.

Finally, the network bits cannot be all 0's, since 0 is not an allowed network address, and is used to indicate an "unknown network or address."

Loopback Address

The network address 127.*x.x.x* has been designated as a local loopback address. The purpose of this address is to provide a test of the local host's network configuration. Using this address provides an internal loopback test of the protocol stack, as opposed to using the host's actual IP address, which would require a network connection.

Local Broadcast

When all the bits in an IP address are set to 1's, the resulting address, 255.255.255.255, is used to send a broadcast message to all hosts on the local network. This configuration at the network layer is mirrored by a corresponding hardware address that is also all ones. Generally this hardware address will be seen as FFFFFFFFFFFF. Routers do not usually pass these types of broadcasts unless specifically configured to do so.

All-Hosts Broadcast

If we set all the host bits in an IP address to 1's, this will be interpreted as a broadcast to all hosts on that network. This is also called a *directed broadcast*, and can be passed by a router if configured to do so. Sample all-host broadcast addresses would look like 132.100.255.255 or 200.200.150.255.

All-Subnets Broadcast

Another type of directed broadcast can be achieved by setting all the subnet address bits to 1's. In this case, a broadcast would be propagated to all subnets within a network. All-subnets broadcasting is rarely implemented in routers.

Identifying Address Classes

The class of an IP address can be determined by looking at the first (most significant) octet in the address. The bit pattern associated with the highest-order bits determines the address class. The bit patterns also define the range of decimal values for the octet that are associated with each address class.

Class A

With a Class A address, eight bits are allotted to the network address, and 24 bits to host addresses. If the highest bit in the first octet is a 0, the address is a Class A address. This corresponds to possible octet values of 0–127. Of these, both 0 and 127 have reserved functions, so the actual range is 1–126. There are only 126 possible networks that are Class A, since only eight bits are reserved for the network address, and the first bit must be a 0. However, with 24 bits available for host numbers, each network can have 16,777,213 hosts.

Class B

With a Class B address, 16 bits are allotted to the network address, and 16 bits to host addresses. A Class B address is characterized by a bit pattern of 10 at the beginning of the first octet. This corresponds to values from 128–191. Since the first two bits are predefined, there are actually 14 bits available for unique network addresses, so the possible combinations yield 16,383 networks, with each network accommodating 65,533 hosts.

Class C

Class C addresses allocate 24 bits to the network address, leaving 8 bits for host addresses. A Class C address will have a bit pattern of 110 leading the first octet, which corresponds to decimal values from 192–223. With a Class C address, only the last octet is used for host addresses, which limits each network to a maximum of 254 hosts per network. Since there are 21 bits available for unique network numbers (three bits are already preset to 110), there are 2,097,151 possible networks.

Class D

Class D addresses have a bit pattern that begins with 1110. This translates into octet values from 224–239. These addresses are not used for standard IP addresses. Instead, a Class D address refers to a group of hosts, who are registered as members of a *multicast group.* A multicast group is similar to an e-mail distribution list. Just as you can address a message to a group of individuals using a distribution list name, you can send data to a group of hosts by using a multicast address. Multicasting requires special routing configuration; it is not forwarded by default.

Class E

If the first four bits of the first octet are 1111, the address is a Class E address. These are addresses that start with 240–254. This class of address is not used for conventional IP addresses. This address class is sometimes referred to as the experimental or research class.

The bulk of our discussion will focus on address Classes A, B, and C, since these are the classes used for routine IP addressing. Table 3-1 summarizes the characteristics of address classes.

Importance of the Subnet Mask

An IP address cannot exist without an associated subnet mask. The subnet mask defines how many of the 32 bits that make up an IP address are used to define the network, or the network and associated subnets. The binary bits in the subnet mask form a filter that only passes that portion of the IP address that should be interpreted as the network address. The process by which this is done is called *bitwise ANDing*. Bitwise ANDing is a logical operation performed on each bit in the address, and the corresponding mask bit. The results of the AND operation are as follows:

```
1 AND 1 = 1
1 AND 0 = 0
0 AND 0 = 0
```

So the only time this operation yields a 1 value is when both input values are 1.

From the example shown in Table 3-2, we can see that an IP address of 189.200.191.239 with a subnet mask of 255.255.0.0 is interpreted as the address of a host on the 189.200.0.0 network, which has a host address of 191.239 on that network. To help you see the relationship of the bits and

TABLE 3-1	Address Class	Bit Pattern in the First Octet	Range of Addresses
IP Address Ranges, Classes, and Bit Patterns	Class A	0xxxxxxx	1–126
	Class B	10xxxxxx	128–191
	Class C	110xxxxx	192–223
	Class D	1110xxxx	224–239
	Class E	1111xxxx	240–254

the dotted decimal notation, the table shows the addresses and masks in both binary and decimal form. A quick way of doing these conversions is to use the Windows Calculator in scientific mode. It will translate between binary and decimal formats.

Each class of IP network has a *default subnet mask*, which defines how many bits of an IP address, for each address class, will represent the network address with no subnetting. These default masks are shown in Table 3-3.

Converting Between Binary and Decimal

In order to manage IP addresses, it is necessary to become intimately acquainted with the process of converting between binary and decimal equivalents. Just as the position of a digit in a decimal number indicates its value in powers of 10, the position of a bit in a binary number indicates its value in powers of 2, as described in Table 3-4. In other words, each bit value doubles as the bit position moves from right to left. This table only goes as far as eight bits (one octet). To extend this table, we would simply add bits to the left, with each new bit having a value double that of the previous bit.

Decimal to Binary Conversion

In order to convert a decimal number to its binary equivalent, the first step is to find the *highest-order* binary bit that will fit into the number. The highest-order bit means the bit position with the greatest decimal value. The decimal value of this bit is subtracted from the number, and

| TABLE 3-2 | How the Subnet Mask Determines the Network Address |

	1ˢᵗ **Octet**	2ⁿᵈ **Octet**	3ʳᵈ **Octet**	4ᵗʰ **Octet**
IP Address	10111101 (189)	11001000 (200)	10111111 (191)	11101111 (239)
AND (each bit)				
Subnet Mask	11111111 (255)	11111111 (255)	00000000 (0)	00000000 (0)
Result				
Network address	10111101 (189)	11001000 (200)	00000000	00000000

TABLE 3-3		Default Subnet Masks, Maximum Networks, and Hosts			
Address Class	**Default Subnet Mask**	**Network Bits**	**Networks**	**Host Bits**	**Hosts**
Class A	255.0.0.0	8	126	24	16,777,206
Class B	255.255.0.0	16	16,383	16	65,533
Class C	255.255.255.0	24	2,097,151	8	254

then the highest-order bit that fits into this remainder is determined. This process is repeated until the remainder is 0. All intervening bit positions are set to 0.

As an example, let's convert the decimal 178 to binary.

1. Looking again at Table 3-4, we can see that the highest-order bit that will fit into 178 is the 128 (2^7). The next higher bit would be 256 (2^8), which will not fit into 178.

2. $178 - 128 = 50$.

3. Looking again at the table, the highest bit that will fit into 50 is 32 (2^5).

4. $50 - 32 = 18$.

5. The highest bit that will fit into 18 is 16 (2^4).

6. $18 - 16 = 2$

7. This remainder fits exactly into the 2 (2^1), leaving a remainder of 0.

TABLE 3-4			Bits and Associated Decimal Values in an Octet					
	Bit 7	**Bit 6**	**Bit 5**	**Bit 4**	**Bit 3**	**Bit 2**	**Bit 1**	**Bit 0**
Binary Bits	1	1	1	1	1	1	1	1
Power of 2	2^7	2^6	2^5	2^4	2^3	2^2	2^1	2^0
Decimal	128	64	32	16	8	4	2	1

TABLE 3-5			Converting 178 Decimal to 1011001 Binary					
	Bit 7	Bit 6	Bit 5	Bit 4	Bit 3	Bit 2	Bit 1	Bit 0
Decimal	128	0	32	16	0	0	2	0
Binary Bits	1	0	1	1	0	0	1	0

This process we just went through is summarized in Table 3-5.

Binary to Decimal Conversion

To convert from binary to the decimal equivalent needed to express an IP address or a subnet mask, it is simply necessary to associate the decimal values with each bit expressed in a binary number, and then to add these decimal values together. This process is shown in Table 3-6, as we convert a binary number, 10011011, to its decimal equivalent.

TABLE 3-6				Converting 10011011 Binary to 155 Decimal					
Bit Pattern	1	0	0	1	1	0	1	1	Decimal Values
	128								128
		0							0
			0						0
				16					16
					8				8
						0			0
							2		2
								1	1
								TOTAL	155

FROM THE CLASSROOM

Powers of 2—some numbers you really need to know

The most confusing aspect of IP addressing for students to grasp is how to determine where the subnet boundaries lie when the mask does not coincide with an octet boundary. An IP address is a 32-bit number that we represent by using four decimal numbers, each representing eight bits of the 32. This is more convenient to write (who wants to write out 32 1's and 0's, anyhow?), and certainly keeps the decimal numbers we need to know to a minimum, but it can be difficult to see how the subnets and their host addresses are organized. In order to be fluent with this, you will need to spend a lot of time looking at binary numbers and powers of two. I hope I can give you a few ideas that will help you home in on the most important things to know.

The numbers you need to know by heart right now are the powers of two from 2^0 to 2^7, and just six others: 192, 224, 240, 248, 252 and 254. How did I get those six numbers? By adding powers of two, starting at the most significant bit in the IP address octet. Let's work out the binary, and watch the pattern as it develops:

- 10000000 in binary equals 128 in decimal.
  This is the value of 2^7.

- 11000000 in binary equals 192 in decimal.
  This is the sum of the values of 2^7 and 2^6.

- 11100000 in binary equals 224 in decimal.
  This is the sum of the values of 2^7, 2^6 and 2^5.

- 11110000 in binary equals 240 in decimal.
  This is the sum of the values of 2^7, 2^6, 2^5, and 2^4.

- 11111000 in binary equals 248 in decimal.
  This is the sum of the values of 2^7, 2^6, 2^5, 2^4, and 2^3.

- 11111100 in binary equals 252 in decimal.
  This is the sum of the values of 2^7, 2^6, 2^5, 2^4, 2^3, and 2^2.

- 11111110 in binary equals 254 in decimal.
  This is the sum of the values of 2^7, 2^6, 2^5, 2^4, 2^3, 2^2, and 2^1.

- 11111111 in binary equals our friend 255, who needs no further explanation.

FROM THE CLASSROOM

These are the only numbers you will ever see in subnet masks, so if you know these you have the subnet masks licked.

Now we need to determine the actual boundaries of the subnets. If the masking is on the octet boundary, it's easy. So let's look at an example that isn't so straightforward.

Take the network 172.16.0.0 with a subnet mask of 255.255.252.0. What are the valid subnet numbers we can use, and the ranges of IP addresses within them?

If there's an octet where the mask is neither all zeros nor all 1's, this is where you need to focus your attention. In this example, the third octet is of interest to us. Work out the binary for this mask: 252 is represented in binary by 11111100. In order to find the first valid subnet number we need to look at the least-significant bit that is a one in our subnet mask. The value of that bit position within the octet, in terms of powers of 2, is 4. So our first valid subnet number is 172.16.4.0. To get the remaining subnet numbers, we just need to count up by fours: 172.16.8.0, 172.16.12.0, 172.16.16.0, 172.16.20.0, all the way up to 172.16.251.0, which is the last of the 63 valid subnet numbers in this example. If our mask

happened to be 255.255.248.0 instead, our third-octet mask would be 11111000 in binary, and we would start with 172.16.8.0 as our first subnet, and count up by 8's instead of 4's, because the value of the last bit position that is a 1 in the mask is 8.

The last thing to find out is the range of host addresses for each subnet. We won't use all 0's or all 1's, because those are reserved for the network number and the directed broadcast. So our first host address for the first subnet is 172.16.4.1, and the last 1 is 172.16.7.254. Where did the 7 in that third octet come from? Remember, the two least significant bits in the third octet are part of the host number, so they need to be included in the counting. Host addresses for the next subnets would be 172.16.8.1 through 172.16.11.254, 172.16.12.1 through 172.16.15.254, and so on.

One last hint for learning about subnets: work out some other examples for yourself, and don't be afraid to write out the binary numbers if you need to!

—*By Pamela Forsyth, CCIE, CCSI, CNX*

CERTIFICATION OBJECTIVE 3.02

Subnetting and Subnet Masks

Up to this point, we have discussed the structure of an IP address, which contains both a network address and a host address. The portion of the IP address reserved for the network address is indicated by the subnet mask. We also discussed that, for each class of address, there is a default number of bits in the subnet mask. All bits not reserved for use as the network address can be used to indicate specific hosts on the network. We will now discuss how we can further segment a network into subnets by borrowing host address bits, and using them to represent a portion of our network.

Purpose of Subnetting

On a single network, the amount of traffic is proportional to the number of hosts, and the sum of the traffic generated by each host. As the network increases in size, this traffic may reach a level that overwhelms the capacity of the media, and network performance starts to suffer. In a wide-area network, reducing unnecessary traffic on the WAN links is also a major issue.

In looking at such problems, it is typical to discover that groups of hosts tend to communicate routinely with each other, and communicate less frequently outside their group. These groupings may be dictated by common usage patterns of network resources, or may be imposed by geographic distances that necessitate slow WAN links between LANs. By using subnets, we can segment the network, thus isolating the groups' traffic from each other. To communicate between these segments, a means must be provided to forward traffic from one segment to another.

One solution to this problem is to isolate the network segments using a bridge between them. A bridge will learn which addresses reside on each side of itself by looking at the MAC address, and will only forward packets that need to cross network segments. This is a quick and relatively inexpensive solution, but lacks flexibility. For example, a bridge would get confused if it found that it could reach a given address on either side of itself. This makes it generally impossible to build redundant pathways using bridges. Bridges also pass broadcasts.

A more robust solution is to use routers that direct traffic between networks, by using tables that associate network destinations with specific ports on the router. Each of these ports is connected to the source network, the destination network, or some intermediate network that leads to the ultimate destination. By using routers, we can define multiple pathways for data, enhancing the fault tolerance and performance of the network.

One solution to addressing in a routed network might be to simply give each network segment a different network address. This would work in an isolated network, but would not be desirable if the network were connected to the outside world. To connect to the Internet, we must have a unique network address, which must be assigned by a regulating agency. These network addresses are in great demand, and in scarce supply. We also increase the complexity of routing data from the public network to our internal networks if we don't have a common point of entry via a single network address.

To gain the economy and simplicity of a single network address, yet provide the capability to internally segment and route our network, we use subnetting. From the standpoint of external routers, our network would then appear as a single entity. Internally, however, we can still provide segmentation through subnets, and use internal routers to direct and isolate traffic between subnets. The following section will discuss the role of the subnet mask in defining subnets.

Adding Bits to the Default Subnet Mask

We have already learned that an IP address must be interpreted within the context of its subnet mask. The subnet mask defines the network address portion of the address. Each class of address has a default mask, which for Class A is eight bits, Class B is 16 bits, and Class C is 24 bits in length.

If we want to subnet a network, we add some number of bits to this default subnet mask, which reduces the number of bits used for the host address. The number of bits we add to the mask determines the number of subnets we can configure. Therefore, in a subnetted network, each address contains a network address, a subnet portion, and a host address.

The subnet bits are taken from the highest-order contiguous bits of the host address, and will start at an octet boundary, since the default masks always end on an octet boundary. As we add subnet bits, we count from the left to right, and convert to decimal using the values associated with their bit positions.

The number of subnets derived from each additional subnet bit is summarized in Table 3-7. Note that the smallest number of useful subnet bits is two, since we cannot use all ones or all 0's for our subnet ID. Also, the maximum number of bits must still leave at least two bits for the host address, due to a similar restriction on all 0's and all 1's.

TABLE 3-7	**Bits Added to Default Mask**	**Decimal Value**	**Number of Subnets**
Subnet Bits, Mask Formats, and Number of Subnets Provided	1	128	0
	2	192	2
	3	224	6
	4	240	14
	5	248	30
	6	252	62
	7	254	126
	8	255	254
	9	255.128	510
	10	255.192	1022
	11	255.224	2046
	12	255.240	4094
	13	255.248	8190
	14	255.252	16,382
	15	255.254	32,766
	16	255.255	65,534

CERTIFICATION OBJECTIVE 3.03

Subnet Planning

The process of subnet planning involves analyzing the traffic patterns on the network to determine which hosts should be grouped together in the same subnet. We also need to look at the total number of subnets that we will need, generally projecting some growth factor for a safety margin. We will also need to consider the class of network address we are working with, and the total number of hosts per subnet that we anticipate having to support.

Choosing a Subnet Mask

In choosing a subnet, the chief consideration is how many subnets we will need to support. The challenge, of course, is balancing the number of subnets with the maximum number of hosts per subnet. There are only 32 bits available for network, subnet and host portions of the address. If we choose a subnet mask that offers more subnets than we need, this will reduce the potential hosts we can support.

The other consideration in choosing the mask is to remember the restriction on subnet values that are all 0's, or all 1's. This most often causes problems with a number like 31 subnets. While this is less than the 32 combinations we could achieve with five subnet bits, it would represent an illegal bit combination, since it would be all 1's. We must therefore use six bits, which yields up to 62 available subnets.

For help in choosing an appropriate subnet mask based on the number of subnets, refer back to Table 3-7.

Impact on the Number of Hosts

Remember that the bits we use for subnetting are subtracted from the bits available to be assigned as host addresses. Each binary bit represents a power of 2, so each bit we take away will cut the potential hosts per subnet in half. Since the address class defines the maximum number of host bits, each class of address is impacted differently by subnetting.

Therefore, if given a network design with a certain number of subnets, proposed hosts per subnet, and a certain class of address, we may find that we have to use fewer subnets, support fewer hosts, or choose a different address class to meet our needs. For each class, the impact of subnetting on the number of hosts is outlined in Table 3-8.

Determining Address Ranges for Each Subnet

Once we have determined the appropriate subnet mask, the next challenge is to determine the address of each subnet, and the allowable range of host addresses on each subnet. The addresses for each of the subnets can be determined by looking at the lowest-order bit of the subnet mask. The value of this bit is the first subnet available. Since we cannot have a subnet ID whose bits are all 0's (this subnet address is reserved), setting all bits but this first one to 0 results in the lowest subnet ID.

The interval range between the subnet IDs will also be equal to the value of the lowest subnet bit. This relates to the powers of 2 associated with the bits. If the lowest bit is a 16, the next bit value above it is a 32. Each time we increment the bits, the subnet value changes by the value of the lowest bit. This will continue up to the subnet value of all 1's, which is not useable, since it is a broadcast address.

In Table 3-9, assume a network address of 135.120.0.0 with a subnet mask of 255.255.224.0.

Table 3-10 summarizes the process of determining subnet address values, and the interval between the subnets.

TABLE 3-8	Subnet Bits	Class A Hosts	Class B Hosts	Class C Hosts
	0	16,777,212	65,531	254
Hosts per Subnet, Based on Mask and Address Class	2	4,194,303	16,382	62
	3	2,097,147	8190	30
	4	1,048,574	4094	14
	5	524,286	2046	6
	6	262,142	1022	2
	7	131,070	510	N/A
	8	65,533	254	N/A

<table>
<tr><td>TABLE 3-9

Determining Subnet Addresses</td><td>

Subnet Bit Pattern	Subnet Value	Subnet Address	Comments
000	0	135.120.0.0	Not available
001	32	135.120.32.0	
010	64	135.120.64.0	
011	96	135.120.96.0	
100	128	135.120.128.0	
101	160	135.120.160.0	
110	192	135.120.192.0	
111	224	135.120.224.0	Not available

</td></tr>
</table>

Once we have determined the addresses of each of the subnets, we can then determine the range of host addresses that are allowed within each subnet. The following example shows the guidelines used to determine the address range.

1. The first available host address is one bit higher than the subnet ID. In other words, if the subnet was 120.100.16.0, the first host address would be 120.100.16.1.

2. Assuming we are using four bits for subnetting, the next higher subnet address would be 120.100.32.0. If we subtract one bit from

<table>
<tr><td>TABLE 3-10

Determining Useable Subnet Addresses for a Given Mask</td><td>

Subnet Bits	First Subnet	Interval Between Subnets	Number of Subnets
2	64	64	2
3	32	32	6
4	16	16	14
5	8	8	30
6	4	4	62
7	2	2	126
8	1	1	254

</td></tr>
</table>

TABLE 3-11	Function	Example	Guideline for Determining Value
Determining Address Ranges for Subnets	First subnet address	120.100.16.0	Net.Work.Subnet.0
	First host	120.100.16.1	Net.Work.Subnet.1
	Last host	120.100.31.254	Next Subnet Address –2
	Subnet broadcast	120.100.31.255	Next Subnet Address –1
	Next subnet address	120.100.32.0	Net.Work.Subnet + Interval.0

this address, we obtain the broadcast address for the lower (16) subnet. This would be the address 120.100.31.255.

3. The highest available host address is one less than the broadcast address, or 120.100.31.254.

These guidelines are summarized in Table 3-11.

CERTIFICATION OBJECTIVE 3.04

Complex Subnetting

So far, we have confined our discussion of subnets to straightforward examples using classful IP addresses. This section will introduce more complex subnetting issues and practices. We will start off by considering subnet masks that cross octet boundaries, since these are frequently a source of confusion. We will also consider variable-length subnet masking (VLSM) as a means of gaining more flexibility in using subnet masks. Finally, we will consider a practice called supernetting, which could be described as subnetting in reverse, since we remove bits from the default subnet mask, rather than adding them.

Crossing Octet Boundaries with Subnet Bits

Whenever we use more than eight bits for subnets, we run into the issue of crossing octet boundaries. One challenge of dealing with these subnet masks is to keep straight the prohibitions concerning all 1's and all 0's. To do this, we have to simultaneously be aware of the subnet bits as an isolated collection of bits, as well as remembering their bit positions, and associated values, in the 32-bit address.

When we cross octet boundaries with a subnet mask, the top eight bits, which consume an entire octet, will have an interval of 1 between subnets. This means any bit combination of 0–255 is permitted in this octet, as long as the additional subnet bits in the lower octet are not also all 1's. At the same time, the bits in the lower octet will increment in values specified by the lowest significant bit in the lower octet. To see how this looks, review Table 3-12, which gives a sample of some of the subnet IDs associated with a Class A network (2.0.0.0) using 10 subnet bits (mask 255.255.192.0).

Variable-Length Subnet Masking

When we define a subnet mask, we have made the assumption that this single mask is going to be consistently used throughout our network. In many cases, this leads to a lot of wasted host addresses, since our subnets may vary widely in size. One prime example of this is where we have a subnet that connects two routers via their serial ports.

There are only two hosts on this subnet—one for each port—but we will have to allocate one entire subnet to these two interfaces. If we could take one of our subnets, and further divide it into a second level of subnetting, we could effectively "subnet the subnet" and retain our other subnets for more productive uses. This idea of "subnetting the subnet" forms the basis for VLSM.

TABLE 3-12	Subnet ID	Subnet Bit Values	Comments
Samples of Subnet IDs Using 10 Subnet Bits	2.0.64.0	0000 0000 01	First subnet ID
	2.0.128.0	0000 0000 10	Next subnet
	2.0.192.0	0000 0000 11	Lower octet bits all ones
	2.1.0.0	0000 0001 00	Lower octet bits all zeros
	2.255.0.0	1111 1111 00	Upper octet bits all ones
	2.255.128.0	1111 1111 10	Last legal subnet

We have talked about an IP address having both a network address portion and a host address portion. With subnetting, we also have a portion of the address devoted to the subnet ID. Collectively, the masked bits representing the network and subnet IDs can be called the *prefix*. Routers can be generically said to route based on prefix. If there were a way to convey specific prefix information with an address, we could override the network-wide assumptions made on the basis of our single subnet mask. To accomplish this, we add explicit information on the prefix to each address reference. The format used to express this prefix (subnet mask) is called the *bitcount* format, which is added to the address using a trailing slash followed by a decimal number. For example, a reference to a Class B address would be represented as 135.120.25.20 /16. The /16 defines 16 subnet bits, equating to the default mask, 255.255.0.0 (16 bits).

To use VLSM, we generally define a basic subnet mask that will be used to divide our first-level subnets, and then use a second-level mask to subdivide one or more of the primary subnets. VLSM is only recognized by newer routing protocols such as EIGRP or OSPF. When using VLSM, all subnet IDs, including the all-ones and all-zeros subnets, will be valid. Figure 3-3 illustrates the concept of VLSM.

Supernetting

In the introduction to this chapter, we referred to RFC 791 as the document that defined the standards for IP addressing. Part of this standard

---

FIGURE 3-3

Using variable-length subnet masks

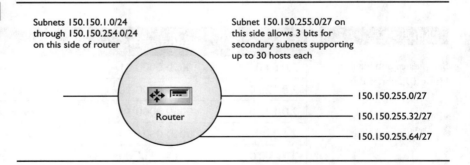

Subnets 150.150.1.0/24 through 150.150.254.0/24 on this side of router

Subnet 150.150.255.0/27 on this side allows 3 bits for secondary subnets supporting up to 30 hosts each

Router

150.150.255.0/27
150.150.255.32/27
150.150.255.64/27

established the address classes and classful addressing. Implied in classful addressing is the assumption that we know what the default subnet mask is, based on the first octet of the address. However, prior to RFC 791, an earlier RFC (760) had proposed an IP address format that was not class based. Address classes were considered a good idea in 1982, since the class assumptions eliminated having to send masking information with an IP address, but since we are now running out of registered IP addresses, the classes have become a serious problem.

The only available addresses that have not been assigned are the Class C addresses. Since a Class C network can only support 254 hosts, large organizations wishing to have a registered address may request multiple contiguous Class C addresses, and integrate them into a single entity using a process called supernetting. It is also sometimes referred to as classless interdomain routing (CIDR).

What supernetting does is to remove bits from the default mask, starting at the right-most bits and working to the left. To see how this works, let's look at an example.

Suppose we have been assigned the following Class C network addresses:

200.200.192.0
200.200.193.0
200.200.194.0
200.200.195.0

With the default mask of 255.255.255.0, these are separate networks. However, if we were to use a subnet mask of 255.255.192 instead, each of these networks would appear to be part of the 200.200.192.0 network, since all the masked bits are the same. The lower-order bit patterns in the third octet become part of the host address space.

Like VLSM, this technique involves a departure from the standard IP address classes. We have discussed these addressing options to provide a sample of the alternatives that have arisen in response to the limitations of classful addressing. When preparing to take the test, remember to focus on a thorough understanding of standard, class-based IP addressing.

FROM THE CLASSROOM

IP: The Next Generation

IP addressing is at a crossroads. The explosive growth of the Internet has caused a crisis with existing IP address formats. The only registered IP addresses that can be obtained right now are Class C addresses. As we have learned, these have severe limitations in terms of the maximum number of hosts supported, which has led to creative approaches such as supernetting.

The longer-term solution is to revamp the whole specification for IP addressing. The proposed solution is called IP version 6, or Ipv6 for short. The format for version 6 IP addresses will move from the present 32-bit

address to an address format of 128 bits. This will be represented as 32 hexadecimal digits, expressed as shown in this example:

```
A923.FF23.BA56.34F3.
```

Unfortunately, this address format is not compatible with existing IP addresses. Ipv6 will probably be implemented first with external IP addresses on the Internet, which would then be routed through gateways to internal networks that continue to use the existing 32-bit address format.

— *By John Pherson, MCSE, MCT, MCNE, CNI*

CERTIFICATION OBJECTIVE 3.05

Configuring IP Addresses with Cisco IOS

The focus of this section will be to take what we have learned about IP addressing and determine how to implement our IP addressing scheme on a Cisco router, using commands from the Cisco IOS command set. The syntax of the commands is shown in each section header, to help you remember them.

Setting IP Addresses and Parameters

The set of parameters we are about to discuss have to do with setting the IP address and subnet masks on the router interfaces, as well as global and per-line settings for how we will express our subnet mask.

ROUTER> TERMINAL IP NETMASK-FORMAT {*bitcount, decimal, or hex*}

This command is issued from the first-level prompt of the privileged or EXEC mode, which is designated by the # prompt. What it does is to define a global format we will use to view subnet masks during the current session. If we do not set this parameter, the default is to use the dotted decimal format.

Examples of the different formats are

Bitcount: /24 (used for classless IP addressing)
Decimal: 255.255.255.0
Hexadecimal: 0xFFFFFF00

ROUTER(CONFIG-LINE)# IP NETMASK-FORMAT {*bitcount, decimal, or hex*}

This command does the same thing as the preceding command, only in this case we are defining the netmask format for a specific terminal line. To get to this command,

1. Enter the EXEC mode.

2. Issue the command ROUTER# CONFIGURE TERMINAL. This puts us at the prompt Router(config)#.

3. From here, type **line** {aux or console or vty 0 4} to get to the line you wish to configure.

4. You will then see the prompt Router(config-line)#, and you can issue the command listed.

ROUTER(CONFIG-IF)# IP ADDRESS *address subnet-mask*

This command is also issued after you have selected an interface and entered the interface configuration mode shown by the Router(config-if)# prompt. This command assigns the IP address to a router interface, and both the address and subnet-mask portions must be specified. The format for the subnet-mask would have been assigned using the last command we discussed.

Host Name to Address Mappings

Host name to address mappings is a process that allows user-friendly names for network hosts, rather than having to specify them by their IP address. When we use these types of names, some method must be provided to convert from the names to the actual IP addresses. This would typically involve using a mapping file or table, and/or a server called a Domain Name Service (DNS) server.

When an address has been resolved from a host name, a router keeps that information in a local cache. This way it can avoid resubmitting the resolution request to the DNS server again later.

ROUTER(CONFIG)# IP HOST *hostname* [*tcp-port-number*] ADDRESS {*ip addresses*}

This command is issued from the global configuration prompt. It is used to add a mapping entry to the host cache used by the router for name-to-address resolution. It requires that you specify the name of the host, and also the IP address (or addresses) associated with that host. It also allows you to specify a TCP port number. If you don't use this parameter, the entry will default to TCP port 23, used for Telnet connections to that host.

ROUTER(CONFIG)#IP DOMAIN-NAME *domain name*

This command is used to specify the default domain name that will be added by the Cisco IOS to an incomplete or "unqualified" host name. A fully qualified domain name (FQDN) would be

server 1.abc.com

where server1 is the host in a domain called abc.com.

If we choose to refer to this server only as server1, then IOS will append the default domain name to the host name for the purpose of submitting a name resolution request to a DNS server.

ROUTER(CONFIG)# IP NAME-SERVER {*name server ip addresses*}

This command is also issued from the global configuration prompt. It is used to specify the address (or addresses) of DNS servers that are available to the router for name-to-address mapping. Up to six name server addresses can be specified with a single command. If this parameter is not used, the router will use 255.255.255.255 (local broadcast address) to find the server.

ROUTER(CONFIG)# (NO) IP DOMAIN-LOOKUP

This command simply turns name resolution on and off. The default is on, with the name server address specified as a local broadcast.

ROUTER# SHOW HOSTS

To avoid "reinventing the wheel," the router will request a name-to-address once, and then keep that information in a local cache. This will shorten the time required the next time the name needs to be resolved. This command will display the contents of this local cache, along with information about the source of the entry (static or resolved by DNS, for example), and its status and age.

Using Ping

Ping (packet Internet groper) is a common utility used with IP to test connectivity between two IP hosts. It operates by sending a set of test packets using ICMP (Internet Control Message Protocol). These packets echo back to the source, showing whether the destination was reachable, and displaying some timing and timeout statistics.

Simple Ping

Simple ping is a command available in the user mode on a Cisco router. It would use the following syntax:

```
Router> ping 131.199.130.3
```

The most common response symbols returned are

!	Successful echo
.	Timed out waiting
U	Destination unreachable
&	TTL exceeded

It will also summarize the results of sending five packets in a success rate percentage. If a ping is successful, it shows that the network protocol is working at least up to the network layer, and that two hosts can successfully connect up to that layer.

Extended Ping

Sometimes the defaults built into simple ping are insufficient to provide the testing desired. If this is the case, an extended PING command is provided in the EXEC command mode in IOS. This version of ping is interactive, and offers the capability to specify the number and size of test packets, the timeout value, and even data patterns, in response to various prompts. You can access this command by entering the EXEC mode, and typing **Router# ping** and pressing RETURN.

You will then be prompted for your settings. You can also access a help file for this command by typing **Router# ping ?** and pressing RETURN.

Using IP TRACE and Telnet

For those occasions when we need more than the PING command to test the operation of the network, there are a few other tools we can use. We may be interested not just in the fact that we can get packets from a source to destination host, but also in the route taken by the packets. We might also be interested in testing host connectivity at protocol layers higher than the network layer. For these tests, we can use IP TRACE for route information, and Telnet, a terminal emulation program that will validate connectivity at higher protocol levels.

Telnet

Telnet is not primarily a testing utility. The purpose of Telnet is to provide a means to emulate a terminal connection into a host system. However, since Telnet is an application that runs at the top of the protocol stack, it can be used to verify the proper functioning of all the intervening layers. Telnet can be used from the user mode in IOS by typing **Router>telnet** {IP address or hostname} or simply the name/address of the host.

IP TRACE

To issue this command, you may be in user mode or EXEC mode (for extended TRACE). Type **Router> trace** {*host name*} **or** {*IP address*}.

In response, this utility will send out three test probes that will discover any routers on the path. It will list the IP address of each router, host name (if it can be resolved), and the return times for each of the three probes.

This list should conclude with the host name or address of the destination host originally specified.

CERTIFICATION SUMMARY

In this chapter we learned that an IP address is a 32-bit address, specified using dotted decimal notation (for example, 125.125.125.100). IP addresses are interpreted using a subnet mask, which defines which portion of the 32 bits represent the network address, and which represent a host number on that network.

IP address classes are assigned based on the value of the first octet of the IP address. These classes range from Class A through Class E. Only Classes A, B, and C are used for normal IP addressing. Each class of address has a default subnet mask, which defines the number of networks and the number of hosts per network for a given address class.

By adding bits to the right of the default subnet mask, we can segment a network into subnets. Subnetting uses bits that were originally reserved for host addresses, thus reducing the number of hosts possible in each subnet.

The following rule applies to the formation of network addresses, subnet IDs, and host numbers: The bit configuration cannot be all 1's or all 0's. All

0's would indicate a network, not a specific address. All 1's would represent broadcasts.

The addresses of subnets on a subnetted network are determined by taking the least significant bit in a subnet mask as the first subnet, and incrementing by the value of that bit. Host addresses on each subnet range from one above the subnet ID to two less than the value of the next higher subnet. One less than the next subnet ID would be a broadcast address for the lower subnet.

Cisco IOS provides commands that will configure the IP addresses of each router interface. Additional commands set the display format for the subnet mask. Several commands configure IP address-to-name translation for the router. Other commands are available for testing the IP configuration, including PING, TRACE, and Telnet.

TWO-MINUTE DRILL

❑ The IP protocol is used for end-to-end routing of data across a network, which may mean that an IP packet must travel across multiple networks, and may cross several router interfaces to get to its destination.

❑ The implementation of address classes divided the address space into a limited number of very large networks (Class A), a much larger number of intermediate-sized networks (Class B), and a very large number of small networks (Class C).

❑ The 32-bit structure of an IP address is comprised of both a network address and a host address.

❑ The concept of *subnetting* extends the network portion of the address to allow a single network to be divided into a number of logical sections (subnets).

❑ Certain addresses in the IP address space have been reserved for special purposes, and are not normally allowed as host addresses.

❑ When all the bits in the host portion of an IP address are set to 0, it indicates the network, rather than a specific host on that network.

❑ The network address 127.*x.x.x* has been designated as a local loopback address. The purpose of this address is to provide a test of the local host's network configuration.

❑ When all the bits in an IP address are set to ones, the resulting address, 255.255.255.255, is used to send a broadcast message to all hosts on the local network.

❑ If you set all the host bits in an IP address to 1's, this will be interpreted as a broadcast to all hosts on that network. This is also called a *directed broadcast.*

❑ The class of an IP address can be determined by looking at the first (most significant) octet in the address.

❑ If the highest bit in the first octet is a 0, the address is a Class A address.

❑ A Class B address is characterized by a bit pattern of 10 at the beginning of the first octet.

❑ A Class C address will have a bit pattern of 110 leading the first octet, which corresponds to decimal values from 192–223.

❑ Class D addresses have a bit pattern that begins with 1110. A Class D address refers to a group of hosts, who are registered as members of a *multicast group.*

❑ If the first four bits of the first octet are 1111, the address is a Class E address.

❑ An IP address cannot exist without an associated subnet mask. The subnet mask defines how many of the 32 bits that make up an IP address are used to define the network, or the network and associated subnets.

❑ You can further segment a network into subnets by borrowing host address bits, and using them to represent a portion of our network.

❑ To gain the economy and simplicity of a single network address, yet provide the capability to internally segment and route our network, use subnetting.

❑ In a subnetted network, each address contains a network address, a subnet portion, and a host address.

❑ The process of subnet planning involves analyzing the traffic patterns on the network to determine which hosts should be grouped together in the same subnet.

❑ In choosing a subnet, the chief consideration is how many subnets you will need to support.

❑ Once you have determined the appropriate subnet mask, the next challenge is to determine the address of each subnet, and the allowable range of host addresses on each subnet.

❑ Whenever you use more than eight bits for subnets, you run into the issue of crossing octet boundaries.

❑ If you could take one of our subnets, and further divide it into a second level of subnetting, you could effectively "subnet the subnet" and retain our other subnets for more productive uses. This idea of "subnetting the subnet" forms the basis for VLSM.

❑ Supernetting removes bits from the default mask, starting at the right-most bits and working to the left.

❑ Host name-to-address mapping is a process that allows user-friendly names for network hosts, rather than having to specify them by their IP address.

❑ Ping (packet Internet groper) is a common utility used with IP to test connectivity between two IP hosts.

❑ You can use IP TRACE for route information, and Telnet, a terminal emulation program that will validate connectivity at higher protocol levels.

SELF TEST

The following Self-Test questions will help you measure your understanding of the material presented in this chapter. Read all the choices carefully, as there may be more than one correct answer. Choose all correct answers for each question.

1. What is the network address for the address 96.2.3.16?

   A. 96.2.0.0

   B. 96.2.3.0

   C. 96.0.0.0

   D. Can't tell

2. What class of address is 190.233.27.13?

   A. Class A

   B. Class B

   C. Class C

   D. Class D

3. How many bits are in the default subnet mask for the address 219.25.23.56?

   A. 8

   B. 16

   C. 24

   D. 32

4. How many hosts are supported by a Class C network address, without subnetting?

   A. 254

   B. 65,000

   C. 255

   D. 16,000

5. What is the default mask for a Class B network?

   A. 255.0.0.0

   B. 255.255.255.0

   C. 255.255.0.0.

   D. 255.225.0.0

6. Approximately how many unique networks are possible with a Class B address?

   A. 254

   B. 16K

   C. 65K

   D. 2M

7. What is the decimal value of the binary number 11001011?

   A. 203

   B. 171

   C. 207

   D. 193

8. What is the binary value of the decimal number 219?

   A. 11101011

   B. 01011101

   C. 11101011

   D. 11011011

9. Subnet bits are added to_____ to segment the network into subnets.

   A. The network address

B. The default subnet mask

C. The host address

D. The subnet ID

10. If eight bits were allocated to subnetting with a Class B address, how many subnets would be possible?

A. 62

B. 256

C. 254

D. 16K

11. Given the subnet mask 255.255.240 on a Class A address, how many bits are allocated to subnetting?

A. 4

B. 5

C. 9

D. 12

12. If the subnet mask for the network 150.25.0.0 is 255.255.224.0, which of these is a valid host address?

A. 150.25.0.27

B. 150.25.30.23

C. 150.25.40.24

D. 150.25.224.30

13. What is the first subnet ID for the network 25.0.0.0 with a subnet mask of 255.192.0.0?

A. 25.192.0.0

B. 25.64.0.0

C. 25.128.0.0

D. 25.192.64.0

14. What is the maximum number of subnet bits possible with a Class C address?

A. 6

B. 8

C. 14

D. 12

15. Given the address 220.195.227.12 with a subnet mask of 255.255. 224.0, what advanced subnetting technique is being used?

A. Subnetting across octets

B. VLSM

C. Supernetting

D. None

16. Given a subnet mask of 255.255.240, which of these addresses is not a valid host address?

A. 150.150.37.2

B. 150.150.16.2

C. 150.150.8.12

D. 150.150.49.15

17. How many hosts per subnet are possible with a Class B address, if five bits are added to the default mask for subnetting?

A. 510

B. 512

C. 1022

D. 2046

18. If you were issued a Class C address, and needed to divide the network into seven

subnets, with up to 15 hosts in each subnet, what subnet mask would you use?

A. 255.255.255.224

B. 255.255.224

C. 255.255.255.240

D. None of the above

19. What IOS command would you issue to set the IP address on a terminal line?

A. ROUTER(CONFIG-IF)# IP ADDRESS

B. ROUTER(CONFIG-LINE)#IP ADDRESS

C. Router(config)#ip address

D. None of the above

20. What IOS command would you use to define the subnet mask for an interface on the router?

A. ROUTER(CONFIG-IF)# IP ADDRESS

B. ROUTER# TERM IP-NETMASK FORMAT

C. Router(config-line)# ip netmask-format

D. Router(config)# ip subnetmask

21. What IOS command turns off name-to-address resolution?

A. ROUTER# NO IP DOMAIN-LOOKUP

B. ROUTER(CONFIG)# NO IP DOMAIN-LOOKUP

C. Router(config-if)# no ip domain-lookup

D. Router(config)# domain-lookup off

22. To view name-to-address mappings cached on the router, what IOS command would you issue?

A. ROUTER> SHOW HOSTS

B. ROUTER(CONFIG)# SHOW HOSTS

C. Router# ip name-server

D. Router(config)# ip name-server

23. If you received a !!!!! in response to a PING command, what would that indicate?

A. Destination unreachable

B. Successful echoes

C. Timeout

D. None of the above

24. Given an IP address of 125.3.54.56, without any subnetting, what is the network number?

A. 125.0.0.0

B. 125.3.0.0

C. 125.3.54.0

D. 125.3.54.32

25. The network 154.27.0.0 can support how many hosts, if not subnetted?

A. 254

B. 1024

C. 65,533

D. 16,777,206

26. Which of the following is a legitimate IP host address?

    A. 1.255.255.2

    B. 127.2.3.5

    C. 225.23.200.9

    D. 192.240.150.255

27. What is the significance of the address 3.255.255.255?

    A. It is a host number

    B. It is a local broadcast

    C. It is a directed broadcast

    D. It is an illegal address

28. How many bits are in the default subnet mask for a Class D network?

    A. 8

    B. 16

    C. 24

    D. None

29. A bit pattern of 1111 leading the first octet of an address would imply what class of network?

    A. Class A

    B. Class B

    C. Class C

    D. Class D

    E. Class E

30. What is the binary equivalent of the decimal 234?

    A. 11101010

    B. 10111010

    C. 10111110

    D. 10101111

31. What is the decimal equivalent of 01011100?

    A. 96

    B. 92

    C. 84

    D. 154

32. The purpose of subnetting is to:

    A. Segment and organize a single network at the network layer

    B. Divide a network into several different domains

    C. Allow bridging between network segments

    D. Isolate groups of hosts so they can't communicate

33. Subnetting is achieved by the following actions:

    A. Subtracting bits from the default subnet mask

    B. Subtracting bits from the network address

    C. Adding bits to the host address

    D. Adding bits to the default subnet mask

34. If we add four bits to the default mask, what is the number of subnets we can define?

    A. 16

    B. 15

    C. 14

D. 12

35. What is the maximum number of subnet bits we can add to a default mask?

A. 8 bits

B. 16 bits

C. 30 bits

D. Depends on address class

36. What is the subnet mask we would use with a Class B address that has three subnet bits added?

A. 255.255.240.0

B. 255.255.224.0

C. 255.224.0.0

D. 255.255.248.0

37. What would be the subnet mask if we added 12 subnet bits to a default Class A subnet mask?

A. 255.255.255.240

B. 255.255.240.0

C. 255.240.0.0

D. 255.225.224.0

38. Given a subnet mask of 255.255.255.0 with a Class B address, how many subnets are available?

A. None

B. 254

C. 16K

D. 65K

39. What happens to the number of hosts per subnet each time we add an additional subnet bit?

A. Hosts are not affected.

B. Available hosts are decreased by two.

C. Hosts per subnet is approximately halved.

D. Hosts per subnet is doubled.

40. In order to accommodate seven subnets, how many subnet bits are required?

A. 3

B. 4

C. 6

D. 7

41. If we included six subnet bits in the subnet mask for a Class C address, how many hosts would each network support?

A. 254

B. 30

C. 4

D. 2

42. What class of address would we have to use if we needed 2,000 subnets, with over 5,000 users each?

A. Class A

B. Class B

C. Class C

D. Class D

43. Given a subnet address of 140.125.8.0, with a subnet mask of 255.255.252.0, what is the subnet address of the next higher subnet?

A. 140.125.16.0

B. 140.125.17.0

C. 140.125.32.0

D. 140.125.12.0

44. Given a subnet address of 5.32.0.0 and a subnet mask of 255.224.0.0, what is the highest allowed host address on this subnet?

A. 5.32.255.254

B. 5.32.254.254

C. 5.63.255.254

D. 5.63.255.255

45. If we saw the following subnet addresses, what would be the subnet mask associated with these subnets?
140.120.4.0
140.120.8.0
140.120.12.0
140.120.16.0

A. 255.255.252.0

B. 255.252.0.0.

C. 255.255.248.0

D. 255.255.4.0.

46. Given the network 2.0.0.0 with a subnet mask of 255.255.224.0, which of these is not a valid subnet ID for this network?

A. 2.255.192.0

B. 2.0.224.0

C. 2.0.16.0

D. 2.254.192.0

47. What is the subnet mask for an address expressed as 175.25.0.0/24?

A. 255.255.0.0

B. 255.255.255.0

C. Depends on address class

D. 255.255.24.0

48. VLSM allows us to

A. Use different subnet masks in different parts of the network

B. Divide a subnet into secondary subnets

C. Use classless IP addressing

D. Both A and B

49. What class of IP address is usually associated with supernetting?

A. Class A

B. Class B

C. Class C

D. Class D

50. Supernetting modifies the default subnet mask in what way?

A. Adds bits to the default subnet mask

B. Adds bits to the network address

C. Removes bits from the subnet ID

D. Removes bits from the default subnet mask

51. What is the appropriate prompt from which to enter the IP ADDRESS command?

A. Router>

B. Router#

C. Router(config-if)#

D. Router(config)#

52. Which of the following subnet mask formats do Cisco routers support?

    A. Dotted decimal

    B. Hexadecimal

    C. Bitcount

    D. All of the above

53. To configure a name-to-address mapping in the router mapping table, you would issue which of the following commands?

    A. ROUTER(CONFIG-IF)# IP HOST

    B. ROUTER(CONFIG-LINE)#IP NAME-SERVER

    C. ROUTER(CONFIG)#IP HOST

    D. Both A and C

54. When a PING command returns a series of periods, what does that indicate?

    A. Success

    B. Non-existent address

    C. Timeout

    D. Unreachable

55. Which of these commands could verify the operation of the protocol stack all the way to the Application layer?

    A. PING

    B. TRACE

    C. Extended PING

    D. Telnet

56. To perform an extended ping to address 1.1.1.1, you would issue which of the following commands?

    A. ROUTER> PING 1.1.1.1

    B. ROUTER# PING 1.1.1.1

    C. ROUTER(CONFIG)# PING

    D. ROUTER# PING

57. The length of an IP address is:

    A. 24 bits

    B. 16 bits

    C. 32 bits

    D. 48 bits

58. Which of the following classes is used for multicasting?

    A. Class A

    B. Class B

    C. Class E

    D. None of the above

59. Which of the following statements is true regarding IP host addresses?

    A. The host address part of an IP address can be set to "all binary 1's" or to "all binary 0's."

    B. The subnet address part of an IP address can not be set to "all binary 1's"or to "all binary 0's."

    C. The network address part of an IP address can be set to "all binary 1's" or to "all binary 0's."

60. An IP address reserved for loopback test is

    A. 164.0.0.0

    B. 130.0.0.0

    C. 200.0.0.0

    D. 127.0.0.0

61. An IP address used for local broadcasting (broadcasting to all hosts on the local network) is

    A. 127.255.255.255

    B. 255.255.255.255

    C. 164.0.0.0

    D. 127.0.0.0

62. An IP address of 100.1.1.1 represents which class of network?

    A. Class B

    B. Class C

    C. Class A

    D. Class E

63. The Class D IP address pattern begins with

    A. 1111

    B. 110

    C. 010

    D. 1110

64. The number 174 is represented in binary form by

    A. 11001110

    B. 10101110

    C. 10101010

    D. 10110010

65. The subnet mask in conjunction with an IP address defines

    A. A multicast address

    B. A host address

C. The portion of the address that should be considered the network ID

D. None of the above

66. The purpose of using subnets is

    A. To divide a network into smaller subnetworks

    B. To improve network performance due to increased traffic

    C. To make the internetwork more manageable

    D. All of the above

67. The default subnet mask for Class B network is

    A. 8 bits long

    B. 24 bits long

    C. 16 bits long

    D. 32 bits long

68. To add bits to a default subnet mask, the bits are taken from

    A. The lowest-order contiguous bits of the host address

    B. The lowest-order contiguous bits of the host address

    C. The highest-order contiguous bits of the host address

    D. The highest-order contiguous bits of the host address

69. In planning subnets, the factors that need to be considered are

    A. The number of subnets needed

    B. The number of hosts per subnet

C. The possible growth in number of subnets or hosts per subnet

D. All of the above

70. How many subnets for Class B are possible if six bits are added to the default mask?

A. 14

B. 30

C. 62

D. 510

71. The value 24 after / in the IP address 135.120.25.20/24 is called

A. A robbed bit

B. A default bit

C. A prefix

D. A host bit

72. An IP address of 199.119.99.1/24 defines

A. 24 subnet mask bits for Class A network

B. 24 subnet mask bits for Class B network

C. 24 subnet mask bits for Class C network

D. 24 subnet mask bits for Class E network

73. What IOS command would you use to define a global format to view the subnet mask during the "current session"?

A. ROUTER # IP ADDRESS

B. ROUTER # TERM DOMAIN-LOOKUP

C. ROUTER # SET FORMAT

D. ROUTER # TERM IP NETMASK-FORMAT

74. The router command ROUTER(CONFIG)# IP HOST {*hostname address*} is used for

A. Viewing the route the packet has taken from source to destination.

B. Viewing the host name and host address.

C. Adding a static mapping of a host name to an address in the router's host cache.

D. Showing source destination network's interfaces with other networks.

75. The maximum number of name server addresses that can be specified using the ROUTER(CONFIG)# IP NAME-SERVER command is

A. Four

B. Six

C. Five

D. Three

76. The following is a response to the ROUTER > PING 120.1.1.2 command

.!!!!

Success rate is 80 percent (4/5), round trip min/avg/max = 28/75/112 ms

The success rate 80 percent in this response means:

A. Four out of five times, the response came back.

B. Five packets were received at destination, and four were received at the source.

C. Four times out of five, there was no response.

D. Four packets out of a total of five packets reached the IP address 120.1.1.2.

77. A user on a Washington, D.C. network receives the following response after issuing a router command:

   Tracing the route to Honolulu
   1Tokyo(127.893.81.2) 800 ms 6 ms
   4 ms
   2 Lisbon(141.925.64.7) 600 ms 8 ms
   6 ms
   Honolulu(151.666.59.4) 400 ms 10 ms
   8 ms
   Washington dc#

This response was most likely obtained by issuing the command:

A. ROUTER# TELNET 151.666.59.4)

B. LISBON# SHOW IPROUTE

C. WASHINGTONDC# SHOW IPROUTE

D. WASHINGTONDC# TRACE HONOLULU

E. HONOLULU# SHOW IP ROUTE

78. For an IP address of 165.3.34.35, netmask of 255.255.255.224, and a subnet ID of 165.3.34.32, the usable host address range is

A. From 165.3.34.34 to 165.3.34.64

B. From 165.3.34.35 to 165.3.34.65

C. From 165.3.34.33 to 165.3.34.62

D. From 165.3.34.33 to 165.3.34.63

Custom Corporate Network Training

Train on Cutting Edge Technology
We can bring the best in skill-based training to your facility to create a real-world hands-on training experience. Global Knowledge has invested millions of dollars in network hardware and software to train our students on the same equipment they will work with on the job. Our relationships with vendors allow us to incorporate the latest equipment and platforms into your on-site labs.

Maximize Your Training Budget
Global Knowledge provides experienced instructors, comprehensive course materials, and all the networking equipment needed to deliver high quality training. You provide the students; we provide the knowledge.

Avoid Travel Expenses
On-site courses allow you to schedule technical training at your convenience, saving time, expense, and the opportunity cost of travel away from the workplace.

Discuss Confidential Topics
Private on-site training permits the open discussion of sensitive issues such as security, access, and network design. We can work with your existing network's proprietary files while demonstrating the latest technologies.

Customize Course Content
Global Knowledge can tailor your courses to include the technologies and the topics which have the greatest impact on your business. We can complement your internal training efforts or provide a total solution to your training needs.

Corporate Pass
The Corporate Pass Discount Program rewards our best network training customers with preferred pricing on public courses, discounts on multimedia training packages, and an array of career planning services.

Global Knowledge Training Lifecycle
Supporting the Dynamic and Specialized Training Requirements of Information Technology Professionals

- Define Profile
- Assess Skills
- Design Training
- Deliver Training
- Test Knowledge
- Update Profile
- Use New Skills

College Credit Recommendation Program
The American Council on Education's CREDIT program recommends 53 Global Knowledge courses for college credit. Now our network training can help you earn your college degree while you learn the technical skills needed for your job. When you attend an ACE-certified Global Knowledge course and pass the associated exam, you earn college credit recommendations for that course. Global Knowledge can establish a transcript record for you with ACE, which you can use to gain credit at a college or as a written record of your professional training that you can attach to your resume.

Registration Information

COURSE FEE: The fee covers course tuition, refreshments, and all course materials. Any parking expenses that may be incurred are not included. Payment or government training form must be received six business days prior to the course date. We will also accept Visa/ MasterCard and American Express. For non-U.S. credit card users, charges will be in U.S. funds and will be converted by your credit card company. Checks drawn on Canadian banks in Canadian funds are acceptable.

COURSE SCHEDULE: Registration is at 8:00 a.m. on the first day. The program begins at 8:30 a.m. and concludes at 4:30 p.m. each day.

CANCELLATION POLICY: Cancellation and full refund will be allowed if written cancellation is received in our office at least six business days prior to the course start date. Registrants who do not attend the course or do not cancel more than six business days in advance are responsible for the full registration fee; you may transfer to a later date provided the course fee has been paid in full. Substitutions may be made at any time. If Global Knowledge must cancel a course for any reason, liability is limited to the registration fee only.

GLOBAL KNOWLEDGE: Global Knowledge programs are developed and presented by industry professionals with "real-world" experience. Designed to help professionals meet today's interconnectivity and interoperability challenges, most of our programs feature hands-on labs that incorporate state-of-the-art communication components and equipment.

ON-SITE TEAM TRAINING: Bring Global Knowledge's powerful training programs to your company. At Global Knowledge, we will custom design courses to meet your specific network requirements. Call 1 (919) 461-8686 for more information.

YOUR GUARANTEE: Global Knowledge believes its courses offer the best possible training in this field. If during the first day you are not satisfied and wish to withdraw from the course, simply notify the instructor, return all course materials, and receive a 100% refund.

In the US:

CALL: 1 (888) 762-4442

FAX: 1 (919) 469-7070

VISIT OUR WEBSITE:

www.globalknowledge.com

MAIL CHECK AND THIS FORM TO:

Global Knowledge

Suite 200

114 Edinburgh South

P.O. Box 1187

Cary, NC 27512

In Canada:

CALL: 1 (800) 465-2226

FAX: 1 (613) 567-3899

VISIT OUR WEBSITE:

www.globalknowledge.com.ca

MAIL CHECK AND THIS FORM TO:

Global Knowledge

Suite 1601

393 University Ave.

Toronto, ON M5G 1E6

REGISTRATION INFORMATION:

Course title _____

Course location _____   Course date _____

Name/title _____   Company _____

Name/title _____   Company _____

Name/title _____   Company _____

Address _____   Telephone _____   Fax _____

City _____   State/Province _____   Zip/Postal Code _____

Credit card _____   Card # _____   Expiration date _____

Signature _____

LICENSE AGREEMENT

THIS PRODUCT (THE "PRODUCT") CONTAINS PROPRIETARY SOFTWARE, DATA AND INFORMATION (INCLUDING DOCUMENTATION) OWNED BY THE McGRAW-HILL COMPANIES, INC. ("McGRAW-HILL") AND ITS LICENSORS. YOUR RIGHT TO USE THE PRODUCT IS GOVERNED BY THE TERMS AND CONDITIONS OF THIS AGREEMENT.

LICENSE: Throughout this License Agreement, "you" shall mean either the individual or the entity whose agent opens this package. You are granted a non-exclusive and non-transferable license to use the Product subject to the following terms:

(i) If you have licensed a single user version of the Product, the Product may only be used on a single computer (i.e., a single CPU). If you licensed and paid the fee applicable to a local area network or wide area network version of the Product, you are subject to the terms of the following subparagraph (ii).

(ii) If you have licensed a local area network version, you may use the Product on unlimited workstations located in one single building selected by you that is served by such local area network. If you have licensed a wide area network version, you may use the Product on unlimited workstations located in multiple buildings on the same site selected by you that is served by such wide area network; provided, however, that any building will not be considered located in the same site if it is more than five (5) miles away from any building included in such site. In addition, you may only use a local area or wide area network version of the Product on one single server. If you wish to use the Product on more than one server, you must obtain written authorization from McGraw-Hill and pay additional fees.

(iii) You may make one copy of the Product for back-up purposes only and you must maintain an accurate record as to the location of the back-up at all times.

COPYRIGHT; RESTRICTIONS ON USE AND TRANSFER: All rights (including copyright) in and to the Product are owned by McGraw-Hill and its licensors. You are the owner of the enclosed disc on which the Product is recorded. You may not use, copy, decompile, disassemble, reverse engineer, modify, reproduce, create derivative works, transmit, distribute, sublicense, store in a database or retrieval system of any kind, rent or transfer the Product, or any portion thereof, in any form or by any means (including electronically or otherwise) except as expressly provided for in this License Agreement. You must reproduce the copyright notices, trademark notices, legends and logos of McGraw-Hill and its licensors that appear on the Product on the back-up copy of the Product which you are permitted to make hereunder. All rights in the Product not expressly granted herein are reserved by McGraw-Hill and its licensors.

TERM: This License Agreement is effective until terminated. It will terminate if you fail to comply with any term or condition of this License Agreement. Upon termination, you are obligated to return to McGraw-Hill the Product together with all copies thereof and to purge all copies of the Product included in any and all servers and computer facilities.

DISCLAIMER OF WARRANTY: THE PRODUCT AND THE BACK-UP COPY OF THE PRODUCT ARE LICENSED "AS IS." McGRAW-HILL, ITS LICENSORS AND THE AUTHORS MAKE NO WARRANTIES, EXPRESS OR IMPLIED, AS TO RESULTS TO BE OBTAINED BY ANY PERSON OR ENTITY FROM USE OF THE PRODUCT AND/OR ANY INFORMATION OR DATA INCLUDED THEREIN. McGRAW-HILL, ITS LICENSORS, AND THE AUTHORS MAKE NO GUARANTEE THAT YOU WILL PASS ANY CERTIFICATION EXAM BY USING THIS PRODUCT. McGRAW-HILL, ITS LICENSORS AND THE AUTHORS MAKE NO EXPRESS OR IMPLIED WARRANTIES OF MERCHANTABILITY OR FITNESS FOR A PARTICULAR PURPOSE OR USE WITH RESPECT TO THE PRODUCT. NEITHER McGRAW-HILL, ANY OF ITS LICENSORS, NOR THE AUTHORS WARRANT THAT THE FUNCTIONS CONTAINED IN THE PRODUCT WILL MEET YOUR REQUIREMENTS OR THAT THE OPERATION OF THE PRODUCT WILL BE UNINTERRUPTED OR ERROR FREE. YOU ASSUME THE ENTIRE RISK WITH RESPECT TO THE QUALITY AND PERFORMANCE OF THE PRODUCT.

LIMITED WARRANTY FOR DISC: To the original licensee only, McGraw-Hill warrants that the enclosed disc on which the Product is recorded is free from defects in materials and workmanship under normal use and service for a period of ninety (90) days from the date of purchase. In the event of a defect in the disc covered by the foregoing warranty, McGraw-Hill will replace the disc.